The Dukan Diet Recipe Book

Dr Pierre Dukan

The Dukan Diet Recipe Book

HODDER &
STOUGHTON

First published in Great Britain in 2010 by Hodder & Stoughton
An Hachette UK company

23

Copyright © 2010 Dr Pierre Dukan

A CIP catalogue record for this title is available from the British Library

ISBN 978 1 444 71035 9

Typeset in Celeste by Hewer Text UK Ltd, Edinburgh

Printed and bound by Clays Ltd, St Ives plc

Hodder & Stoughton policy is to use papers that are natural, renewable
and recyclable products and made from wood grown in sustainable forests.
The logging and manufacturing processes are expected to conform to
the environmental regulations of the country of origin.

Hodder & Stoughton Ltd
338 Euston Road
London NW1 3BH

www.hodder.co.uk

Contents

PREFACE

Taking the next step with the Dukan Diet

I wrote the book that you are now holding in France for the French public and, as perhaps you are aware, this public has two particular cultural features. As well as being one of the countries in the world most attached to its cuisine and the enjoyment of food, France is also home to some of the world's slimmest women.

When my editors asked me to adapt the book for my British readers, to suit your tastes, I did think this was a valid request. However, after some reflection, I decided against it. Why? Because I had not conceived and written this book as a traditional cookery book, focusing solely on flavour and pleasure, but rather as a book that would fit with my golden rules and the 100 foods that make up my diet. And I thought that what a French person on a diet wants could not be any different from what a British person following the same diet might want.

When a man or a woman genuinely wants to lose weight, their main objective, and their greatest pleasure, is to watch the pounds that have been ruining their life melt away. And if at the same time eating can be pleasurable, frustration is silenced and the way is clear for them to achieve their True Weight and keep it.

When I handed over the manuscript for my book, *The Dukan Diet,* to my editor, I was aware that this was the finishing touch to a lifetime's work. This work had been to provide a method, firstly for myself, then for my patients and finally for my future readers, with which to fight weight problems. This is my very own method, which has taken shape over my thirty years of daily medical practice.

When I first started out in the field of nutrition, it was with an innovation that at the time incurred the wrath of my peers, who were initiators and staunch defenders of the idea of low-calorie dieting and weighing out food into tiny quantities. I had set in motion the protein food diet.

I was very young and I could easily have become discouraged, except that the simplicity of this diet, its effectiveness and the way it perfectly suited the psychological profile of overweight people, convinced me that I was indeed on the right track. It was this conviction that held me fast to the mast as my boat faced stormy waters.

By nature I am ingenious, curious and creative and I have used these gifts in the field that I know and practise in best: man's relationship with his weight. As the years have gone by, I designed, then patiently honed, this diet based on daily contact with my patients. Introducing a never-ending toing and froing of tentative measures, I kept only those that improved both the method and the results achieved in the short, medium and, in particular, the long term.

This is how a method took shape that today has become mine. Its impact, the way it has spread and the affectionate messages I receive from my readers give my life meaning. Whatever my hopes and ambitions may have been when writing my first book, I could never have imagined that it would be so well received by such an incredibly wide public. The book has been translated and published in countries as distant as Korea, Brazil and Bulgaria.

How the book spread owed very little to marketing and absolutely nothing to advertising. Strangely enough, it sold itself, being passed on from one person to another, linked in one forum to another forum and, recently, handed on from one doctor to the next. From this, I have concluded that the book contained a fortunate ingredient that, over and above its purely nutritional impact, allowed my presence as a therapist, with my empathy, energy and, possibly, also my experience, to show through.

As I already mentioned, I have received many letters telling me about results, sending warmth and gratitude, but also some letters containing criticism or suggestions. Among the latter, some people wanted my weight-loss programme to include an exercise section and others asked for extra recipes. In the 2010 edition of *The Dukan Diet,* I satisfied this first request with a whole chapter devoted to exercise, where exercise is not simply advised, but formally prescribed as medicine. This book has been written to satisfy the second request.

For this recipe book, which follows the method and instructions found in *The Dukan Diet*, I have been able to draw upon the inventiveness and contributions of all those people who were extra clever at developing recipes while they were on the diet. Thank you.

I would also like to thank Roland Chotard, a French Michelin-starred chef, who read *The Dukan Diet* and lost 60 pounds. In exchange, he has given me his own translation of my recipes, improved by his inventiveness, professionalism and, perhaps even more so, by his desire to lose weight while still enjoying gastronomic delights.

And my thanks must also go to Gaël Boulet, training manager with Alain Ducasse, one of the greatest chefs in the world, for his invaluable advice about how to create simple but inspirational food and how to replace our taste for fats by using spices and seasoning.

WHAT IS THE DUKAN DIET?

Proteins and vegetables – the foundations of my diet

For those of you unacquainted with my programme or diet, my entire method is based around two main food groups:

- foods rich in animal proteins
- vegetables

For me, these two food categories make up the natural foundation of our human diet. My evidence for this is that when our species came into being some 50,000 years ago, our diet consisted of these foods.

Whenever a new species appears, lengthy and reciprocal adaptation takes place between the species that is evolving from the previous one and its environment. A genetic code finding its way must encounter an environment ready and willing to host it. Indeed, it is inconceivable that a species will develop in a geographical space that does not give it exactly what it needs. If there was ONE time in our species' history when our digestive system and the foods available were completely in tune, then it was when we appeared on Earth.

And this is anything but a mere detail. This fact lies at the very heart of my approach, which is to search for points of reference in the study of the human diet, where the belief holds sway that we have a never-ending capacity to adapt and are omnivorous in all places at all times.

Well, actually, no. There are in fact some foods that are more human, more fundamental, than others. This is not an ideological approach advocating that we return to some backward-looking age, but rather a pragmatic one that recognizes how powerful the inclinations are that are part of our very nature.

When our species came into being, man was designed to hunt, to pursue game and catch fish. Women concentrated on gathering whatever foods they could find, especially plants. From this initial matrix, these foods very early on acquired the status of foundation foods, that of being the most specific, the most human, the noblest, densest and most appropriate foods for humans, both with regards to nutrition and to their emotional power (this being infinitely more useful in weight control). What is even more important is that for 50,000 years, these foods have been continually evolving alongside us.

It is clear that humans are not what they were. No longer hunter-gatherers, people have become sedentary, grow crops and breed animals. They have built civilizations and brought the environment under control, to the extent that we take from it exactly what we want, including our food, which is now designed far more to be a source of pleasure than as a way of getting nutrition. By doing this, we have created a new diet, poles apart from what we were designed to eat, and have become addicted to its voluptuous pleasures. Our new diet appeals to the senses and is seductive, rich, luscious, comforting and emotional, but it is a diet that makes us fat.

There are two food groups in our current diet, fats and sugars, that for a long time were found only in foods considered rare and luxurious, but which over the past 50 years have had a dramatic emergence. By definition, these foods with a high fat or sugar content, abundantly available nowadays in supermarkets, are foods of extreme reward, which simply did not exist when our bodies, and in particular our brains, came into being. Nobody ate fats because the animals that were hunted were lean. Nobody ate sugary foods because sucrose did not exist. Even the Sun King, Louis XIV, in the unprecedented luxury of his Versailles palace, never tasted any sugary foods other than fruit and honey.

My intention is not to argue that we return to the caveman's frugal diet, but rather to drive my point home that dieting by going back to eating foods that we originally ate is no hardship.

Waging the war against overeating

I know that most nutritionists advocate that our diet should contain starchy foods, cereals, carbohydrates and good fats. I myself am convinced that slow sugars are useful, but just not during the weight-loss phase. Thirty years of battling at my patients' side have persuaded me that this sort of balanced diet is difficult to keep up when you are trying to lose weight. Suggesting to overweight or obese people that they diet by balancing out food groups with optimum proportions does not take proper account of their psychology and issues.

The weight-loss period is a period of war and to achieve true victory, the result has to be lasting peace. Waging a war without a war effort or without preparing for it is unimaginable. If overweight people were capable of shedding pounds by simply eating a little of everything in a balanced way, they would not have any extra pounds in the first place. Man's eating patterns cannot be understood just through the laws of thermodynamics. This way of explaining excess pounds in terms of energy – people put on weight because they eat too much and exercise too little – is correct, but it explains nothing (or rather it only explains how things happen, but not why they happen).

If you have put on weight – to the extent that this extra weight is troubling you – then eating fulfils a purpose other than feeding yourself. Although I do not know you personally, I can assure you that whatever it is in your diet that has made you put on weight, it is not what you ate to nourish yourself, but rather the extra things you put in your mouth to give yourself some pleasure. And it is this need for pleasure that is the underlying theme, and true explanation, for your weight problem. This urge is so strong it takes you over and drives you to become overweight, even though you condemn it and end up suffering and feeling guilty because of it.

My daily conversations over the years with patients, listening to them and carefully recording their experiences and stories, have convinced me that if a subconscious demand for pleasure like this exists, an urge that is strong enough to drown out reason and silence feelings of guilt, then this is because the person is suffering, temporarily or permanently, from a shortage of other pleasures and other sources of fulfilment.

And generally, what motivates some of you to do something about your weight, to find the energy to wage war against it and forgo the pleasure you had been getting from the comfort eating that caused your weight problem, is that you are expecting other sources of pleasure from other areas in your life. It is the promise of bright spells heralding better days ahead.

During the fragile, uncertain times, what overweight people want is to have something to show for their fight: tangible, visible and sufficiently encouraging results that will strengthen their bullish hopes and motivation, both of which can all so easily ebb away with any sense of stagnation or failure. With this in mind, I have gone for a diet that gets results, but at the same time adheres to my code of ethics as a doctor. This is to look after my patients' interests over the long term, ensuring permanent results and stabilizing weight loss.

How did a diet based on proteins evolve

For those of you not acquainted with my diet and who have not yet read *The Dukan Diet*, the work containing my method, I am here going to briefly summarize what is in my programme and how it works.

The main focus is on proteins. This is where my journey into the world of nutrition started and most of my career as a medical practitioner has been occupied with creating a protein-based diet programme.

In 1970, I introduced the first diet in France based solely on this food group. At the time, I had great difficulty in getting people to agree to singling out one food group because it broke completely with the thinking at the time, when low-calorie diets reigned supreme and unchallenged. Nowadays, my protein diet finally has its place among the weapons we use to tackle weight problems. To my mind though, it still has not found its proper place as the undisputed number one diet. It is the driving force behind any proper diet and should be used just for a few days to launch the rocket because a diet that does not suddenly take off has no life to it.

The prevailing theory, which is extremely conservative and impervious to results and statistics that time and again prove it wrong, still sides with low-calorie dieting and eating all foods in tiny quantities. This is a strategy that has produced, still produces and will for ever more continue to produce greater numbers of fat people each year.

Eminent colleagues who hold firm to this position turn

the debate into a psychiatric analysis. They claim that being deprived of certain foods makes us put on weight, that diets that at the outset lead to dramatic weight loss, especially so for first-time dieters, then find that parallel to the sudden losses comes equally sudden weight gain, often with extra pounds and yo-yoing patterns. Dieting is said to be a sure-fire way of putting on weight.

Such cases exist, I come across them, but they are far from being the rule. They are either due to some daft diet, like eating nothing but soup or the Beverly Hills exotic fruit diet, because of a very long and frustrating low-calorie diet or a powdered protein diet. This last sort of diet is doubly damaging, both for our metabolism by using a 98% pure nutrient, and for our eating patterns, with a diet restricted to industrially manufactured powders.

The common denominator in all these diets, where the weight just goes back on again afterwards, is the total lack on all sides of any stabilization phase. This comes both from those advocating the diets, with their common sense advice such as 'be careful', 'watch what you eat', 'don't overeat' and other token recommendations, and from patients who, wanting to believe in these words and still feeling enthusiastic and happy about having lost weight, consider themselves out of all danger. Quite obviously, both sides are mistaken. Only a proper monitoring programme can prevent failure and rebounds. And this programme must monitor the dieter with precise, concrete and effective rules that are easy to remember and part of a ritual. It is this series of graduated rules and responses, acting as a succession of roadblocks to stop you piling back on the pounds, that proves, as the weeks and months go by, to be enough to control your weight. This is a programme that takes action in a comprehensive, concerted and self-confident way.

Let's wage war against some diets, yes! But not against all diets indiscriminately – that would be throwing the baby out with the bath water. Of all the diets that work too quickly, too violently, too much against human nature, it is the protein powder diets that need to be controlled, or left at any rate in the hands of doctors or psychiatrists.

On this subject, I would like to recount a true story that will no doubt entertain you and tell you all you need to know about what I think of industrial proteins.

During the winter of 1973, my secretary handed me the phone and a stranger with a thick Nordic accent told me how he had bought one of my books, had read it and managed to lose a few stone without too much trouble or suffering.

'I am in Paris, I'd love to come by and shake your hand and thank you in person.'

A few hours later, a huge Norwegian aged about fifty was sat in my office. 'Although you don't know it you changed my life. I wanted to give you a present to thank you.'

And he took a huge, magnificent salmon out of his travelling bag.

'In Norway I have a few salmon farms and this fish, one of the finest specimens from my favourite fjord, has been specially caught for you and wood-smoked according to traditional methods.'

I love salmon, so I thanked him profusely.

'This is nothing, just a little taster from my forests. Here is my real present.'

He then produced from his bag of tricks a plain, cylindrical, aluminium tin the size of a hat box.

'Doctor, do you know what is inside this tin? Your fortune is inside!'

And he took the lid off the tin to reveal a mass of white powder.

'Let me explain. I run many dairies in the Netherlands. We produce butter, but we don't know what to do with the buttermilk, the main by-product, so we feed it to the pigs. Do you know what is in this buttermilk? Soluble milk globules, pure protein! I want to make these tonnes of powdered proteins available to you to be turned into slimming sachets.'

This man was a visionary industrialist. Ten years later, protein powders became the most widely sold slimming product in the world.

'Thank you so much for your salmon, I shall think of you and your fjords as I tuck into it. However, I won't take the tin or the powder inside; this is not how I intend to fight for my proteins. Perhaps you don't realize it, but your first present, your extraordinary salmon, is a source of protein. Just as I love salmon and can already picture myself showing it to my family and enjoying it, the idea of eating this white powder disgusts me. And why should

I try and get my patients and those who trust me to do what I myself don't want to do.'

The four-step programme

To come back to my diet as it is today, it is a programme made up of four successive interconnected diets designed so that they guide the overweight person to their desired weight and keep them there. These four successive diets, which gradually include more foods, have been specially devised to bring about, in the following order:

- With the first diet, a lightning start and an intense and stimulating weight loss.
- With the second diet, a steady, regular weight loss that takes you straight to your desired weight.
- With the third diet, consolidation of this newly achieved but still unstable weight, lasting for a fixed period of time – five days for every pound lost.
- With the fourth diet, permanent stabilization, in return for three simple, concrete, guiding, extremely effective but non-negotiable measures to be followed for the rest of your life: protein Thursdays, no more lifts or escalators and three tablespoons of oat bran *a day*.

Each of these diets has a specific effect and a particular mission to accomplish, but all four draw their force and their graduated impact from using pure proteins:

- Pure proteins only during the Attack phase.
- The proteins are combined with vegetables during the Cruise phase.
- Then, they are eaten with other foods during Consolidation.
- Finally, they are pure again in permanent Stabilization, but only for one day a week.

The Attack phase gets its jump-start, taking the body by surprise, by using the protein diet in its purest form without compromise, for two to seven days, depending on the individual.

It is this same diet that, by alternating proteins, gives power and rhythm to the Cruise phase, which leads you straight to your desired weight.

It is also this same diet, used occasionally, that is the mainstay of the Consolidation phase, the period of transition between hard-line dieting and a return to normal eating.

And finally, it is this diet that, for just one day a week but for the rest of your life, guarantees permanent Stabilization. In exchange for this occasional effort, for the other six days of the week you will be able to eat without guilt or any particular restriction.

If the group of 72 protein-rich foods is the driving force behind my programme and its four successive diets, before you put this into practice, and so that you benefit from all it can offer, we need to describe the particular way this diet works and explain its impressive effectiveness.

How does the pure protein diet work, which is the base and starting point for the other three phases, which will keep your weight stable? All will be explained below.

THIS DIET PROVIDES ONLY PROTEINS

Where Do You Find Pure Proteins?

Proteins form the fabric of living matter, both animal and vegetable, so they are found in most known foods. But to develop its unique action and full potential, the protein diet has to be composed of elements as close as possible to pure protein. In practice, other than egg whites, no food is this pure.

Whatever their protein content, vegetables are still too rich in carbohydrates. The same goes for all cereals, legumes and starchy foods, and for soya beans too, which although known for their protein quality are too fatty and rich in carbohydrates, which means that none of these vegetables can be used here.

The same applies to certain foods of animal origin, more protein-rich than any vegetables, but which are also too high in fat. This is the case with pork, mutton and lamb, some poultry, such as duck and goose, and some cuts of beef and veal.

There are, however, a certain number of foods of animal origin that, without attaining the level of pure protein, come close to it and because of this they will be the main players in the Dukan Diet.

- Beef, except for ribs, spare ribs and cuts used for braising or stewing
- Lean cuts of veal
- Poultry, except for duck and goose
- All fish, including oily fish whose fat helps protect the heart and arteries so they can be included here
- All other seafood
- Eggs, even though the small amount of fat in the yolk taints the purity of the egg white
- Virtually fat-free dairy products. Though very rich in protein and virtually fat-free, they may, nevertheless, contain a small amount of lactose, a natural milk sugar found in milk just as fructose is found in fruit. They can, however, remain in the Dukan Diet's strike force because they have little lactose but lots of taste.

How Do Proteins Work?

The purity of proteins reduces the calories they provide
Every animal species feeds on foods made up of a mixture of the only three known food groups: proteins, carbohydrates and lipids. But for each species, there is a specific ideal proportion for these three food groups. For humans the proportion is 5-3-2, i.e. five parts carbohydrates, three parts lipids and two parts proteins, a composition close to that of mother's milk.

It is when our food intake matches this 'golden proportion' that calories are then most efficiently assimilated in the small intestine so that it is easy to put on weight.

On the other hand, all you have to do is change this ideal proportion and the calories are not absorbed as well and the energy from the foods is reduced. Theoretically, the most radical modification conceivable, which would reduce most drastically the calories absorbed, would be to restrict our food intake to a single food group.

In practice, even though this has been tried out in the USA with carbohydrates (the Beverly Hills diet allowed only exotic fruits) or fats (the Eskimo diet), it is hard to eat only sugars or fats and this has serious repercussions for our health. Too much sugar allows diabetes to develop easily and too much fat, apart from our inevitable disgust, would pose a major risk to the cardiovascular system. Furthermore, proteins are essential for life and if the body does not get them it raids its own muscle for them.

If we are to eat from one single food group, the only possibility is proteins: a satisfactory solution as far as taste is concerned, it avoids the risk of clogging up the arteries and by definition it excludes protein deficiency.

When you manage to introduce a diet limited to protein foods, the body has great difficulty in assimilating the chewed food that it was not programmed to deal with and it cannot use all the calories contained in the food. It finds itself working like a two-speed engine, in a scooter, lawnmower or motor boat, designed to run on a mixture of pure petrol and oil but trying to run on pure petrol. It putters and then stalls, unable to use its fuel.

In the same way, when the body feeds on very high-protein foods it restricts itself to taking the proteins it needs to survive and for the vital maintenance of its organs (muscles, blood cells, skin, hair, nails) and it makes poor and scant use of the other calories provided.

Assimilating proteins burns up a lot of calories
To understand the second property of protein, which makes the Dukan Diet so effective, you need to familiarize yourself with the idea of SDA, or Specific Dynamic Action, of foods. SDA represents the effort or energy that the body has to use to break down food until it is reduced to its basic unit, which is the only form in which it can enter the bloodstream. How much work this involves depends on the food's consistency and molecular structure.

When you eat 100 calories of white sugar, a quick carbohydrate par excellence composed of simple, barely aggregated molecules, it is assimilated very quickly. The work to absorb it burns up only 7 calories, so 93 usable calories remain. The SDA for carbohydrates is 7%.

When you eat 100 calories of butter or oil, assimilating them is a bit more laborious: 12 calories are burned up, leaving only 88 for the body. The SDA of lipids is 12%.

Finally, to assimilate 100 calories of pure protein – egg whites, lean fish, or virtually fat-free cottage cheese – the task is enormous. This is because protein is composed of an aggregate of very long chains of molecules, whose basic links, amino acids, are connected to each other by a strong bond that requires a lot more work to be broken down. It takes 30 calories just to assimilate the proteins, leaving only 70 for the body, i.e. the SDA is now 30%. Assimilating proteins makes the body work hard and is responsible for producing heat and raising our body temperature, which is why swimming in cold water after eating a protein-rich meal is inadvisable as the change in temperature can result in immersion hypothermia.

This characteristic of proteins, annoying for anyone desperate for a swim, is a blessing for overweight people who are usually so good at absorbing calories. It means they can save calories painlessly and eat more comfortably without any immediate penalty.

At the end of the day, after eating 1,500 calories worth of proteins, a substantial intake, only 1,050 calories remain after digestion. This is one of the Dukan Diet's keys and one of the reasons why it is so effective. But that's not all . . .

Pure proteins reduce your appetite
Eating sweet foods or fats, easily digested and assimilated, does create a superficial feeling of satiety, all too soon swept away by the return of hunger. Recent studies have proved that snacking on sweet or fatty foods does not delay your urge to eat again, or reduce the quantities eaten at the next meal. On the other hand, snacking on proteins does delay your urge for your next meal and does reduce the amount that you then eat. What is more, if you only eat protein foods this produces ketonic cells, powerful natural appetite suppressants that are responsible for a lasting feeling of satiety. After two or

three days on a pure protein diet, hunger disappears completely and you can follow the Dukan Diet without the natural threat that weighs down on most other diets: hunger.

Pure proteins fight oedema and water retention
Certain diets or foods are known as being 'hydrophilic', that is, they encourage water retention and the swelling this causes. This is the case for mostly vegetable diets, rich in fruits, vegetables and mineral salts. Protein-rich diets are the exact opposite. They are known as being water-repellent, in that they promote elimination through urine and, as such, provide a welcome purge or 'drying out' for tissues gorged with water, which is a particular problem during the premenstrual cycle or during the pre-menopause.

The Attack diet, made up exclusively of proteins that are as pure as possible, is of all diets the one that best gets rid of water.

This is particularly advantageous for women. When a man gains weight, this is mostly because he overeats and stores his surplus calories in the form of fat. For a woman, how she puts on weight is often more complex and bound up with water retention, which prevents diets from working properly.

At a certain time during the menstrual cycle, in the four or five days before a period starts, or at certain key times in a woman's life, such as puberty, the pre-menopause or even in the prime of her sexual life if she has hormonal disorders, women, and especially those who are overweight, begin to retain water and start to feel spongy, swollen and puffy-faced in the morning. They are unable to remove rings from their swollen fingers; their legs feel heavy and their ankles swell. With this retention they put on weight; usually this is reversible but it can become chronic.

Even women who diet in order to slim down and avoid this swelling are surprised to find that during these periods of hormonal surge all the little things that worked before no longer have any effect. In all these cases, which are not so rare, pure proteins such as are found in my programme's Attack diet have a decisive and immediate effect. In a few days, sometimes even in a matter of hours, water-soaked tissues begin to dry up, leaving a feeling of wellbeing and lightness that shows up immediately on the scales and greatly boosts motivation.

Pure proteins boost your system's resistance
This is a characteristic well known to nutritionists which is also more generally recognized. Before tuberculosis was eradicated through antibiotics, one of the traditional treatments was to overfeed patients by significantly increasing the amount of proteins. At Berck in northern France, one of the top centres for treating tuberculosis, teenagers were even forced to drink animal blood. Today, sports coaches and trainers advocate a protein-rich diet for athletes who demand a lot from their bodies. Doctors give the same advice to

increase resistance to infection, for anaemia or to speed up the healing of wounds.

It is advisable to make use of this advantage, because any weight loss, no matter how small, will weaken the body. I have personally seen that the Dukan Diet's Attack phase, composed exclusively of pure proteins, is the most stimulating phase. Some patients have even told me that it had a euphoric effect, both mentally and physically, and that this happened from the end of the second day.

Pure proteins enable you to lose weight without losing muscle or skin tone

There is nothing surprising in this observation when you realize that the skin's elastic tissue, as well as the body's muscular tissue, is made up essentially of proteins. A diet lacking in proteins forces the body to use its own muscles and the skin's proteins, so that the skin loses its elasticity, to say nothing of menopausal women having brittle bones. Combined, these effects cause ageing of the skin, hair and even general appearance which friends and family soon notice, and which can be enough to make you stop the diet early. Conversely, a protein-rich diet and, even more so, a diet made up exclusively of proteins like the Dukan Diet's first diet, has no reason to attack the body's reserves because the body is being given massive protein supplies. Under these conditions, the weight loss is rapid and toning, muscle firmness is maintained and the skin glows, allowing you to lose weight without looking older.

This particular feature of the Dukan Diet might seem of secondary significance to young and curvy women with firm muscles and thick skin, but it is very important for those women approaching their fifties and therefore the menopause or who have less muscle structure or a fine and delicate skin. This is especially important because, and it has to be said here, there are too many women nowadays who manage their figures guided solely by their scales. Weight cannot and should not be the sole issue. Radiant skin, healthy-looking hair, tissue strength and general body tone are criteria that contribute just as much to a woman's appearance.

Conclusion

The pure protein diet, the initial and principal driving force behind the four integrated diets that make up my programme, is not like other diets. It is the only one to use just a single food group and one well-established category of foods with the highest protein content.

During this diet and throughout the whole programme, any mention of calories and of calorie-counting is to be avoided. Whether a few or many are eaten has little effect on the results. What counts is keeping within this food category. So the actual secret of the programme's first two slimming phases is to eat a lot, even to eat in anticipation, before the hunger pangs take over. Hunger that turns into uncontrollable cravings that can no longer be appeased by the proteins you are allowed to eat leads the careless dieter towards pure comfort foods, foods with little nutritional value, sugary, creamy, rich and destabilizing foods which nevertheless have a strong emotive power.

The effectiveness of this diet is therefore entirely connected with choosing the right foods, as powerful as lightning when intake is limited to this category of food, but if this rule is not followed it slows right down and you have to resort to miserable calorie-counting. To spell it out, by following this diet you have replaced a calories system with a categories system. There is absolutely no need for you to count calories; all you need do is stay within the categories. But if you stray away from the list of permitted foods, you are no longer allowed to eat any quantity you like and you will have to start counting how many calories you eat.

So this is a diet you cannot follow in half measures. It relies on the great all-or-nothing law, which explains not only its metabolic effectiveness, but also its amazing impact on the psychology of an overweight person who also operates according to this same law of extremes.

With a temperament that goes from one extreme to another, just as determined when making an effort and as easy-going when giving up, the overweight person finds in each of the four stages of my programme an approach to suit them perfectly.

These affinities between the individual's psychological profile and the diet's structure create a synergy whose importance is hard for outsiders to understand, but which is decisive for those involved. The mirroring generates a strong bond with the diet that makes losing weight easier, but which really comes into its own in the ultimate Stabilization stage. This is when everything rests on the one day of proteins per week, a day of redemption, a measure that is as specific as it is effective. That on its own, and in this form, can be accepted by anyone who has always struggled with their weight.

THE 100 NATURAL FOODS FOR THE ATTACK AND CRUISE PHASES

Eat as much as you like

My method consists of four phases and I have used this structure to organize the recipes. The first two phases, Attack and Cruise, are responsible for actual weight loss. The next two phases, Consolidation and Stabilization, protect the weight you have chosen and achieved.

Recipes have a vital role to play during the first two phases, which is to offer pleasure, flavour and variety and to satisfy hunger. Afterwards, so much diversity is possible that no single book could contain all the recipes. However, I have not said my final word on the subject and there will be a recipe book for the Consolidation phase, so watch out for it!

In this book you will find only two types of recipes:

- Recipes that we call 'pure protein recipes' because they only use foods with a high protein content. These recipes can be used for all phases of the diet, but are the only recipes to be used in the Attack phase.
- Recipes that combine proteins and vegetables. These recipes can be used in the Cruise phase.

These recipes have been devised based on the 100 foods that make up my diet and there is absolutely no restriction on how much you eat, when and in what combination. You are granted this total freedom on condition that you introduce no other food during the programme's first two phases, which will take you to the weight you want.

In the first two phases of my programme, the 100 foods that you can eat as much as you like of are:

72 Protein foods (Attack)

Meat and offal (16)

Beef steak
Fillet of beef
Sirloin steak
Roast beef
Rump steak
Tongue
Bresaola (air-dried/wind-dried beef)
Veal escalope
Veal chop
Kidney
Calf's liver
Cooked ham slices (without any fat or rind)
Cooked chicken and turkey slices (without any fat or rind)
Fat-reduced bacon
Game (venison, pheasant, partridge, grouse)
Rabbit/Hare

Fish (25)

Cod (fresh)
Dab/Lemon sole
Dover sole
Fish roe (cod, salmon, herring, mullet)
Grey mullet
Haddock
Hake
Halibut
Herring
Mackerel
Monkfish
Plaice
Pollock/Coley
Rainbow trout/Salmon trout
Red mullet
Salmon
Sardines
Sea bass
Sea bream
Skate
Smoked salmon
Swordfish
Tuna
Turbot
Whiting

Seafood (15)

Calamari/Squid
Clams
Cockles
Crab
Crayfish
Dublin Bay prawns
Lobster
Mediterranean prawns/Gambas
Mussels
Oysters
Prawns
Scallops
Seafood sticks (surimi)
Shrimps
Whelks

Poultry (8)

Chicken
Chicken livers
Guinea fowl
Ostrich
Pigeon
Poussin
Quail
Turkey

Eggs (2)

Hen's eggs
Quail's eggs

Virtually fat-free dairy products (5)

Fat-free Greek yoghurt/Fat-free natural yoghurt (plain or flavoured with aspartame)
Virtually fat-free cottage cheese
Virtually fat-free fromage frais
Virtually fat-free quark
Skimmed milk

Vegetable protein (1)

Tofu

28 Vegetables (Cruise)

Artichoke
Asparagus
Aubergine
Beetroot
Broccoli/Purple sprouting broccoli
Cabbage (all types)
Carrot
Celery/Celeriac
Chicory
Courgette
Cucumber

Fennel

French beans/String beans/Mangetout

Leek

Mushroom

Onion

Palm heart

Pepper

Pumpkin/Marrow/Squash

Radish

Rhubarb

Salad leaves (all types)

Soya beans

Spinach

Swede

Swiss chard

Tomato

Turnip

Extras

Oat bran

For years, the first two actual slimming phases in my programme did not contain any starchy foods, any cereals or any flour-based foods. The programme worked fine without them but many of the men and women who followed it eventually ended up longing for carbohydrates.

I discovered oat bran while attending a cardiology conference in America, where there was a presentation on how it reduces cholesterol and diabetes. I brought some home and one morning, having run out of flour, I created a special pancake, which I now call the Dukan oat bran galette, for my daughter, Maya. It is made of oat bran, an egg and some fromage frais or quark, sweetened with aspartame. As she loved it and felt completely full, this spurred me on to suggest to my patients that they try the galette. Their enthusiasm for it persuaded me to include it in my method and my books. This is how oat bran gradually became a fundamental part of my method, the only carbohydrate allowed among the proteins and even within the sanctuary of the Attack phase. Why?

Firstly, from a clinical perspective I very quickly noticed an improvement in results: my patients followed the diet better over the long term; they felt less hungry and full sooner; and all in all were much less frustrated.

I tried to understand how oat bran works and looked at the studies available on it. Oat bran is the fibrous husk that surrounds and protects the oat grain. The grain, used to make rolled oats, is rich in simple sugars. Oat bran is the grain's jacket with few simple sugars but very rich in proteins and particularly in soluble fibres. These fibres have two physical properties which give oat bran its medicinal role.

Firstly, there is its ability to absorb – it can absorb up to 25 times on average its volume of water. This means that as soon as it reaches the stomach, it swells and takes up enough space to make you very quickly feel full. It is also extremely viscous. Once in the small intestine along with food that has by now turned into a pulp, it starts to behave like flypaper and all the surrounding nutrients stick to it. It stops them being absorbed into the blood and it takes some away with it into the stools.

As oat bran makes you feel full up and lose calories, it is a precious ally in my battle against the weight problem epidemic. I say my battle because using oat bran does not take away one of the main advantages my method offers: unlimited access to my 100 foods which you can eat as often and AS MUCH of as you like. Low-calorie diets obviously cannot derive so much benefit from oat bran as they already include starchy foods and even some sugary foods weighed out in limited quantities.

I have done some work of my own to check how oat fibres work. Using coprological studies we can compare the calorie content of the stools of individuals when they have eaten oat bran and when they have not. From this I could see that the brans available were not all as good as each other; and the way bran is produced greatly determines how effective it is. Canada and Finland are the main countries to produce oat bran. I have had the opportunity to work with Finnish agricultural engineers and discovered that two manufacturing parameters, milling and sifting, turned out to be crucial. Milling involves grinding the bran and determines the size of its particles; sifting involves separating the bran from the oat flour.

If the milling is too fine this sterilizes the bran and it loses almost all its effectiveness. Likewise if the bran is too coarse and has not been ground enough its useful surface viscosity is lost. If the bran is not thoroughly sifted it is not sufficiently pure and contains too much flour. However, really thorough sifting makes it too expensive. Working with agricultural engineers and the coprological study of stools, we worked out an effectiveness index for bran to cover milling and sifting which allows its best medicinal effects to develop.

Milling should ideally produce particles with a medium+ size (technically called M2bis). As for sifting, it is after it has been sifted for a sixth time, B6, that oat bran has negligble fast carbohydrate content. These two indexes together make up the overall M2bis-B6 index.

Most manufacturers, and Anglo-Saxon manufacturers in particular, only sell bran to be used in cooking, in porridge for example, which is a real national institution in Britain. They prefer bran to be milled very finely and are not that bothered about the sifting as long as the bran tastes soft and creamy but its medicinal effects are compromised.

Meetings are scheduled at nutrition and dietetics conferences and symposia to discuss this work and to try and reconcile culinary and nutritional needs. I am currently working with international manufacturers and distributors, sharing these results with them to try and get them to adopt the milling-sifting index, which makes production a little more expensive but produces more nutritional bran. In the meantime, the recommended type of bran can be found on our website www. thedukandiet.co.uk.

During the Attack phase, I prescribe a dose of one and a half tablespoons of oat bran per day. I recommend eating it as a savoury galette or sweetened with aspartame and prepared as in the recipes from page 131.

Most of my patients eat their galette first thing, so that they avoid feeling famished mid-morning. Others eat them for lunch with a nice slice of smoked salmon or some thinly sliced dried beef. Other patients have them late afternoon, at the 'danger hour' when cravings can overtake them. Or even after supper when they want to rummage around in cupboards to find a final treat before bedtime. If you would like some more oat bran-based ideas, look on www.allaboutoatbran.com for a whole range of recipes for crêpes, muffins, cakes, pizza bases and oat bran bread.

It should be noted that oat bran galettes are a fantastic weapon against bulimia. My slimming programme is of course not for bulimia sufferers but there may be some who read this book and I know from using oat bran regularly with my patients that it can help them greatly and that they can prepare as many galettes as they want, however they want with the flavours they like, and that this will help them avoid their worst crises when they can consume huge amounts of calories from very poor-quality food.

But even if a person is not bulimic, it is possible to go through difficult periods when irrepressible cravings can put paid to a carefully designed and structured slimming phase. In such unusual circumstances, for a day or two (and I really do mean for a day or two) you can eat more oat bran and up to three galettes per day.

Flavourings

Skimmed milk, either fresh, in cartons or powdered, is allowed and can improve the taste and the consistency of tea or coffee; it can also be used to make sauces, cream desserts, custard tarts and many other dishes.

Sugar is not allowed, but aspartame, the best known and most widely used sweetener in the world, is perfectly acceptable and can be used without restriction, even by pregnant women, which proves just how harmless it is.

Vinegar, spices, herbs, thyme, garlic, parsley, onion, shallots, etc. are not only allowed but highly recommended. Using them brings out the flavour of foods and heightens their sensory value. These oral sensations trigger our nervous system which is responsible for whether we feel full or not, contributing to our feeling of being satisfied. To be clear, I am saying quite simply that spices are not just taste enhancers, which in itself is no small achievement, but that they are foods that encourage weight loss. What certain spices such as vanilla or cinnamon do is offer their warm and reassuring taste in exchange for sugary flavours. Others such as coriander, curry powder, colombo (Caribbean curry spice) powder and cloves can cut down the need for salt, especially for women who suffer from water retention who want to add salt to everything even before they have tasted it.

Gherkins, as well as pickled onions, are allowed as long as they are condiments. If eaten in too large a quantity they become a vegetable and outside the Attack phase's pure protein requirement.

Lemons can be used to flavour fish or seafood, but cannot be consumed as lemon juice or lemonade, even without sugar, because although sour, lemons are still a source of sugar and are therefore incompatible with the programme's first two phases, the Attack and Cruise phases.

Mustard and salt are acceptable but must be used in moderation. This is particularly true when it comes to water retention, common among teenage girls whose periods are irregular and in premenopausal women or women following hormone treatment. There are salt-free mustards and low-sodium diet salts if you want to use them liberally.

Ordinary ketchup is not allowed because it is both very salty and very sweet, but there are sugar-free natural ketchups that can be used in moderation and there are high-quality tomato purées such as the famous Heinz varieties that turn into a real treat with just a little flavouring and spicing up – without any of that sweet after-taste which does not go well with meats.

Fat-reduced cocoa is allowed.

Chewing gum deserves better than this single entry in the extras category. To my mind it is extremely useful in the fight against weight problems and especially so during my programme's first two slimming phases, the

Attack and Cruise phases. I do not usually eat gum myself as chewing is not elegant, but if I am overstressed I do have some then. 'Bruxism' is what dentists call the night-time habit of grinding your teeth until the enamel is worn down. And as a lot of overweight people often eat 'under stress', chewing gum can slow down this mechanical swing towards eating whenever you feel under pressure. What is more, a mouth that is busy chewing gum cannot take or chew anything else so this is a technique for keeping your mouth full. Moreover, there are some sugar-free chewing gums that are absolutely delicious and packed with different flavours, sometimes intense and stimulating flavours. Many scientific studies have also proved at regular intervals how useful chewing gum is when battling against weight problems, diabetes and even tooth decay.

What should we think about the nutritional content of sugar-free chewing gum and which ones should we choose? Of course we are only talking here about so-called sugar-free gum. What this means is that there is no white table sugar or sucrose but the sweeteners used are still sugars and contain almost as many calories as the white variety. Fortunately their ability to sweeten is hundreds of times more powerful than that of ordinary sugar; they are absorbed in the stomach and assimilated very slowly indeed and they have very little effect on insulin and fat storage. Select your sugar-free chewing gum according to taste but go for the ones whose flavour lasts longest in your mouth.

All oil is forbidden. Even though olive oil justifiably has a reputation for protecting the heart and arteries, it is still oil and pure lipids have no place in a pure protein diet.

Apart from these extras and the food categories just described, you may eat NOTHING ELSE. All the rest, anything that is not explicitly mentioned on this list, is forbidden during the Attack diet's relatively brief kick-start period.

Concentrate on what you are allowed to eat and forget the rest. Make sure you get enough variety and pick ingredients for your meals in any order you want so as to keep things interesting. And do not ever forget that all the foods allowed and on this list are for you, really and truly for you.

THIS DIET MUST INCLUDE A LOT OF WATER

The Importance of Drinking Water

The water issue is always a little disconcerting. Opinions and rumours circulate about it, but almost always there is some kind of 'authority' telling you today the exact opposite of what you heard yesterday. However, this water issue is not simply a marketing concept for diets, designed to amuse those who want to lose weight. It is a question of great importance that, despite the enormous combined efforts of the press, doctors, mineral-water manufacturers and simple common sense, has never really totally won over the public and in particular those people on diets.

To simplify things, it may seem essential to burn calories so that our fat reserves melt away; but this combustion, as necessary as it is, is not enough. Losing weight is as much about eliminating as it is about burning.

Would a housewife dream of doing the laundry or washing dishes without rinsing them? It is the same with losing weight and while on this subject it is essential to spell things out. A diet that does not involve drinking a sufficient quantity of water is a bad diet. Not only is it ineffective, but it leads to the accumulation of harmful waste.

Water purifies and improves the diet's results
Simple observation shows us that the more water you drink, the more you urinate and the greater the opportunity for the kidneys to eliminate waste derived from the food burned. Water is, therefore, the best natural diuretic. It is surprising how few people drink enough water.

The many demands in our busy day conspire to delay then finally obliterate our natural feeling of thirst. Days and months go by and the message disappears altogether and no longer plays its part in warning us about tissue dehydration. Many women, whose bladders are smaller and more sensitive than men's, do not drink to avoid having to go to the toilet constantly or because it is awkward at work or on public transport or because they do not like public toilets.

However, what you may get away with under ordinary

circumstances has to change when following a weight-loss diet and if healthy lifestyle advice remains unheeded there is one argument that always wins people over:

Trying to lose weight without drinking is not only toxic for the body, but it can reduce and even completely block the weight loss so that all your work is for nothing. Why? Because the human engine that burns its fat while dieting functions like any combustion engine. Burned energy gives off heat and waste. If these waste products are not regularly eliminated afterwards by the kidneys, they will accumulate and, sooner or later, interrupt combustion and prevent any weight loss, even if you are following the diet scrupulously.

It is just the same for a car engine with a clogged exhaust pipe, or a fire in a fireplace full of ashes. Both end up choking and dying from the build-up of waste. Sooner or later, bad nutrition and the accumulated effects of bad healthcare and extreme or unbalanced diets will make the overweight person's kidneys become lazy. More than anyone else, the overweight person needs large quantities of water to get their excretion organs working again.

At the outset, drinking a lot of water may seem tedious and unpleasant, especially in wintertime. But if you keep it up, the habit will grow on you. Then, encouraged by the pleasant feeling of cleaning out your insides and even better, of losing weight, drinking often ends up once again becoming something you need to do.

When they are combined, water and pure proteins act powerfully on cellulite

This fact only concerns women, as cellulite is a type of fat that, under hormonal influence, accumulates and remains trapped in the most feminine areas of the body: the thighs, hips and knees. Diets are very often powerless against it. I have personally discovered that the pure protein diet, together with a reduction in salt intake and a real increase in consumption of mineral water with a low mineral content, leads to a more harmonious weight loss with moderate but genuine slimming in the difficult areas, such as the thighs or insides of the knees.

Compared to other diets that the patient has followed at different times in her life, this is the combination that for the same amount of weight loss achieves the best overall reduction around the hips and thighs.

These results can be explained by the water-repellent effect of proteins and the intense filtering undertaken by the kidneys made possible by this massive water intake. Water penetrates all tissues, even cellulite. It goes in, pure and clean, and comes out salty and full of waste. Adding the powerful effect of burning up pure proteins to this expulsion of salt and waste brings about definite, even if modest, results. This is a rare achievement and sets the diet apart from most others which have no specific effect on cellulite.

When should you drink water?

People still cling to old wives' tales that would have you believe that it is best not to drink at mealtimes to avoid food trapping the water. Not only does this idea of not drinking at mealtimes have no physiological basis, but in many cases it makes things worse. Not drinking while you eat, at a time when you naturally get thirsty and when drinking is so easy and enjoyable, may result in you suppressing your thirst altogether and then, when you are busy later on with your daily activities, you forget to drink water for the rest of the day. During the Dukan Diet and especially during the alternating proteins phase, except in cases of exceptional water retention caused by hormonal or kidney problems, it is absolutely essential to drink a litre and a half of water a day. If possible drink mineral water or take it in any other liquid form such as tea, herbal tea or coffee.

A cup of tea at breakfast, a large glass of water mid-morning, two more glasses and a coffee at lunch, one glass during the afternoon and two glasses with dinner and you have easily downed a couple of litres. Many patients have told me that in order to drink when they were not thirsty they got into the habit of drinking directly from the bottle and this worked better for them.

Which water should you drink?

- The most suitable waters for the pure protein Attack phase are mineral waters low in sodium, which are slightly diuretic and laxative. Among the best known are Vittel, Evian, Buxton, Highland Spring, Volvic and Perrier, the famous sparkling variety. You should avoid

San Pellegrino and Badoit, which are good but contain too much sodium to be drunk in large quantities.

- If you drink tap water, then continue to do so. It is far more important to drink enough water to get your kidneys working again than it is to worry about what is in the water you are drinking.
- The same holds true for all the various sorts of teas, green teas and herbal teas which can tempt those people who enjoy their cuppa and, in particular, prefer hot drinks especially to warm up in winter.
- In the case of diet fizzy drinks, I consider them all to be great allies in the fight against weight problems (or excess weight) as long as they have no more than one calorie per glass. As far as I am concerned not only do I allow them, but I recommend them and for several reasons. First of all, it is often the best way to make sure you drink the one and a half litres of liquid already mentioned. In addition, they have virtually no calories or sugar. Finally, and above all, a fizzy drink like Diet Coke or Coca Cola Zero, the market-leading brand, provides a clever mix of intense flavours, just like traditional Coke, which can reduce the craving for sugar if used repeatedly by those who like snacking on sweet things. Many of my patients have confirmed that diet fizzy drinks were fun and comforting when used as a part of their diet and actually helped them. The sole exception regarding diet fizzy drinks is in the case of a dieting child or teenager. It has been proven that substituting 'fake' sugar does not work and

barely reduces their craving for sugar. Furthermore, unlimited use of sweet-tasting fizzy drinks might form a habit of drinking without thirst and just for pleasure, which could make them vulnerable to more dangerous addictions later on in life.

Water is naturally filling
As you know, we often associate the sensation of an empty stomach with being hungry, which is not entirely wrong. Water drunk during a meal and mixed with food increases the total volume of the food mass and stretches the stomach, thereby inducing that feeling of a full stomach, the first signs of satisfaction and satiety: yet another reason for drinking at mealtimes. However, experience proves that keeping the mouth busy works just as well in between meals, for example during the danger zone in your day, between 5 p.m. and 8 p.m. A big glass of any liquid will often be enough to calm your hunger pangs.

Nowadays, the world's richest populations are confronting a new type of hunger: a self-imposed denial of food while surrounded by an infinite variety of foodstuffs which they dare not touch because of the risk to their health or because they have weight problems.

It is surprising to see that at a time when individuals, institutions and pharmaceutical laboratories dream of discovering the perfect and most effective appetite suppressant, there are so many people for whom this is an issue who still do not know about or even worse refuse to use a method as simple, pure and inexpensive as drinking water to tame their appetite.

THE DIET HAS TO BE LOW IN SALT

Kicking the Salt Habit

Salt is an element vital to life and present to varying degrees in any and every food. So adding salt at the table is always superfluous. Salt is just a condiment that improves the flavour of food, sharpens the appetite and is all too often used purely out of habit.

A low-salt diet is never dangerous

You could and even should live your whole life on a low-salt diet. People with heart and kidney problems or high blood pressure live permanently on low-salt diets without suffering harmful effects. However, people with low blood pressure and who are used to living that way should exercise caution.

A diet too low in salt, especially when combined with a large intake of water, can increase the filtering of the blood, washing it out and in doing so even reduce its volume and lower blood pressure further and, if already naturally low, this can produce fatigue and dizziness if you get up quickly. These people should not go overboard with salt reduction and should limit their water intake to one and a half litres per day.

On the other hand, too much salt leads to water retention in your body tissue

In hot climates, salt pills are regularly distributed to workers so that they avoid dehydration from the sun. For women, especially women intensely influenced by hormones, during premenstrual or premenopausal periods, or even during pregnancy, many parts of the body become spongy, retaining impressive amounts of water.

For these women, this diet, a water-reduction diet par excellence, works most effectively when as little salt as possible is absorbed, allowing the water to pass more quickly through the body, just as it does during cortisone treatment.

By the way, we often hear people complaining that they have put on two or even four pounds in one evening, after a lapse in their diet. Sometimes a weight gain like this is not even due to a real lapse. When we analyze exactly what was eaten, we can never track down the 18,000 calories of food required to produce these four extra pounds. It was simply the combination of an over-salty meal accompanied by drinks; salt and alcohol combine to slow down the throughput of the water drunk. Never forget that one litre of water weighs two pounds and two teaspoons of salt are enough to retain this water in your body's tissues for a day or two.

This being the case, if during your diet you cannot avoid a professional dinner engagement or family celebration that will force you to put aside the rules you are otherwise following, then at least avoid eating salty foods and drinking too much alcohol. And do not weigh yourself the next morning, because a sudden increase in weight may discourage you and undermine your determination and confidence. Wait until the following day, or even better two days, while stepping up the diet, drinking mineral water with a low mineral content and cutting back on salt. These three simple measures should be enough to get you back on track.

Salt increases appetite; decreasing your salt intake decreases your appetite

This is a simple observation. Salty foods increase salivation and gastric acidity, which in turn increases your appetite. Conversely, lightly salted foods have only a slight effect on digestive secretions and no effect on appetite. Unfortunately, the absence of salt reduces thirst and when you follow the Dukan Diet you have to accept that during the first days you will have to make yourself drink a large amount of liquid so that you boost your need for water and re-establish your natural thirst.

THE RECIPES

For a long time I thought that if I made the results the priority, people were bound to accept putting gastronomy and culinary delights on hold. I had not reckoned with my patients' and readers' ingenuity and unlimited creativity when they feel strongly motivated. They were amazingly inventive within the totally defined and structured framework that I had set them, that of proteins and vegetables, but without any limits on quantity. Over five years, I have received thousands of recipes that use these foods and stick to the rules about how to prepare, combine and alternate them. And I have been amazed to see the extent to which people have been keen to share with others a recipe they really loved.

One day in 2005, I took a phone call from one of my readers who wanted to tell me that, having bought my book by chance in a railway station, he had followed the instructions in it and by himself had lost more than four and a half stone in just over six months.

'I have spent my life working as a chef. I love cooking just as much as I enjoy eating my food, so over the years I had become very overweight. Your programme appealed to me because I'm a great fish and meat eater and, most importantly, I have a huge appetite and your book starts off with the words "as much as you want".

I've drawn upon all my talent and expertise to bring the brilliance of great cooking to the foods that we are freely allowed and to the many recipes in your book. I have been having a feast for six months and I have lost weight without really suffering.

To thank you, I am going to send you these recipes from your repertoire, but that I have adapted for my own pleasure based on your rules, so that your readers and patients who lack time and imagination can enjoy them too.'

As life would have it, apart from being music to my ears, this phone call also struck a chord in my own family. My son Sacha, who was studying dietetics, read these recipes and, together with this great and experienced chef, set up his laboratory and brought out a range of ready-prepared diet dishes, the only range I know of in Europe that is produced without any fat, flour or sugar.

You will find these recipes in this book, along with other recipes, adaptations and variations that are perhaps a little less professional, but every bit as creative, from women who write on the forums and work together with a common goal of losing weight using my method. I take this opportunity to thank, from the bottom of my heart, all those people who use the forums and have helped me by sending in their own versions of my recipes. There are too many of them for me to acknowledge them all, but they will know who they are from the name of their particular forum: aufeminin, supertoinette, mesregimes, dukanons, seniorplanet, doctissimo, zerocomplexe, atoute, cuisinedukan, vivelesrondes, commeunefleur, nouslesfemmes, club-regimes, e-sante, commeunefleur, regimefacile, meilleurduchef, volcreole, forumliker, yabiladi, forme-medecine, actiforum, easyforum, dudufamily . . .

PURE PROTEIN RECIPES

Poultry

AILES DE POULET CROUSTILLANTES
(CRISPY CHICKEN WINGS)

(2 servings)

Preparation time: 10 minutes (plus 2–3 hours
 marinating)
Cooking time: 20 minutes

50ml (2fl oz) soy sauce
1 garlic clove, crushed
1 tablespoon liquid sweetener
4 teaspoons 5-spice powder (star anise, cloves,
 pepper, cinnamon, fennel)
1 teaspoon chopped ginger
6 chicken wings, tips cut off (can be used for stock on
 page xx)

Mix all the ingredients together in a bowl and leave
the chicken wings to marinate for 2–3 hours, turning
them over once or twice. Place in a roasting tin and
cook under the grill for 5–10 minutes until the wings

start to hiss and crackle. Turn the wings over and cook for a further 5–10 minutes until golden brown. Remove the skin before eating.

BOUILLON D'AILERONS DE POULE AUX MOULES (CHICKEN BROTH WITH MUSSELS)

(6 servings)

Preparation time: 30 minutes
Cooking time: 2 hours 5 minutes

1.5kg (3lb 5oz) chicken wing tips
2 onions, peeled
2 shallots, peeled
1 head of garlic, peeled
4 sticks of celery
1 bouquet garni
Salt and black pepper
1kg (2lb 4oz) mussels, scrubbed and rinsed well
6 chives, chopped
6 sprigs of chervil, chopped

Bring 3 litres (5¼ pints) slightly salted water to the boil and add the chicken wing tips, onions, shallots, garlic head, celery, bouquet garni and pepper to the water. Cover the pan and cook for 2 hours over a very low heat, taking care not to overheat because this will make the broth go cloudy. Once the broth is ready, cook the mussels in a high-sided frying pan over a very high heat for about 3 minutes until they open. Discard any unopened mussels. Strain the cooking juices and keep to one side, then shell the mussels, remembering to keep a few back in reserve to garnish the broth. Divide the mussels among six bowls, adding a little of the cooking juices. Strain the cooked broth (removing the chicken wing tips), bring to the boil and add salt and black pepper. To finish, pour the chicken broth over the mussels, sprinkle with the chopped herbs and garnish with the mussels kept back for decoration. Serve immediately.

BOUILLON DE POULET À LA THAÏE (THAI CHICKEN BROTH)

(2 servings)

Preparation time: 15 minutes
Cooking time: 3 hours

2 chicken carcasses
1 onion, cut into quarters
1 bunch of coriander stalks and roots, roughly
    chopped
2 fresh lemongrass stalks (just the white part),
    crushed
2 kaffir lime leaves, chopped (or not)

1 tablespoon chopped galangal (or ginger)
Salt and black pepper

Put the chicken carcasses into a big pan containing 2 litres (3½ pints) cold water. Bring to the boil and skim. Turn down the heat, add the rest of the ingredients to the pan and leave to simmer for 2–3 hours, taking care not to overheat because this will make the broth go cloudy. Strain the broth before serving (the kaffir lime leaves and lemongrass will give this broth a lovely lemony flavour).

BROCHETTES DE POULET À LA MOUTARDE (MUSTARDY CHICKEN KEBABS)

(4 servings)

Preparation time: 20 minutes (plus 2 hours marinating)
Cooking time: 20 minutes

You will need kebab sticks (soak in a little water if using wooden sticks so that they do not burn when the meat is being cooked).

4 chicken breasts
2 tablespoons strong mustard
1 teaspoon lemon juice
½ garlic clove, chopped
1 low-salt chicken stock cube

1 teaspoon cornflour
50ml (2fl oz) skimmed milk

Preheat the oven to 220°C/425°F/Gas 7.
Cut the chicken breasts into big chunks and put them in a large bowl. In another bowl, mix together the mustard, lemon juice, garlic and the stock cube dissolved in 250ml (9fl oz) hot water. Pour three-quarters of this marinade over the chicken, mix thoroughly and refrigerate for 2 hours. After 2 hours, thread the chicken chunks onto kebab sticks and roast them for 15 minutes. Meanwhile, blend the cornflour with the cold milk and add to a small saucepan with the remaining quarter of the marinade. Gently simmer the mixture for 5 minutes so that the sauce thickens and serve alongside the kebabs.

BROCHETTES DE POULET AUX ÉPICES (SPICY CHICKEN KEBABS)
(5 servings)

Preparation time: 30 minutes (plus 2–3 hours marinating)
Cooking time: 10 minutes

You will need 25 small wooden kebab sticks (soak in a little water so that they do not burn when the meat is being cooked).

1kg (2lb 4oz) chicken breasts, cut into cubes
250ml (9fl oz) fat-free natural yoghurt
1 teaspoon chilli powder
1 teaspoon ground turmeric
1 teaspoon ground cumin
1 teaspoon ground coriander
1 teaspoon grated ginger
1 garlic clove, crushed

Prepare the marinade with the yoghurt and all the spices, ginger and garlic. Thread the chicken pieces onto the kebab sticks and place in a dish, covering them completely with the marinade. Leave to marinate in the fridge for several hours or overnight. Place the kebabs under the grill or on the barbecue and cook for 8–10 minutes until the meat is browned and tender.

CUISSES DE POULET EN PAPILLOTES (HERB-STUFFED CHICKEN LEGS)

(2 servings)

Preparation time: 10 minutes
Cooking time: 45 minutes

100g (3½oz) virtually fat-free fromage frais
1 shallot, chopped
1 tablespoon chopped parsley
20 chives, finely chopped

Salt and black pepper
2 chicken legs

Preheat the oven to 150°C/300°F/Gas 2.
Prepare a forcemeat by mixing together the fromage frais, shallot, parsley and chives. Season with salt and black pepper. Remove the skin from the chicken legs and, using a sharp, pointed knife, make an incision into the thickest part of the meat, about 2cm (¾ inch) long and 1.5cm (½ inch) deep. Push the forcemeat into the slits and coat the chicken legs with the rest of the mixture. Cut out two sheets of aluminium foil and place a chicken leg in the centre of each piece, closing them to form a parcel. Put a little water in the bottom of a gratin dish and place the parcels in it. Bake in the oven for 45 minutes.

ESCALOPES DE POULET TANDOORI
(TANDOORI CHICKEN)

(6 servings)

Preparation time: 15 minutes (plus overnight
    marinating)
Cooking time: 25 minutes

6 chicken breasts
3 garlic cloves, crushed
2cm (¾ inch) piece of ginger, very finely chopped

2 green chillies, very finely chopped
300g (10½oz) fat-free natural yoghurt
2 teaspoons tandoori masala
Juice of 1 lemon
Salt and black pepper

Put each chicken breast on a sheet of clingfilm and bat into 1cm (½ inch) thick escalopes. Mix all the other ingredients together, making sure that the garlic, ginger and chillies are really well crushed so that they blend together evenly. Make incisions into the chicken so that the yoghurt-spice mixture can get right inside the flesh and leave the chicken to marinate overnight in the fridge.

The following day, preheat the oven to 200°C/400 °F/ Gas 6.

Cook the escalopes for 20 minutes, then finish them off under the grill so that they turn brown.

ESCALOPES DE VOLAILLE AU CURRY ET YAOURT (BARBECUED CURRY CHICKEN)

(4 servings)

Preparation time: 5 minutes (plus 2 hours marinating)
Cooking time: 5 minutes

You will need a barbecue.

4 chicken breasts
300g (10½oz) fat-free natural yoghurt
3 teaspoons curry powder
Salt and black pepper

Heat up the barbecue. Put each chicken breast on a sheet of clingfilm and bat into 1cm (½ inch) thick escalopes. Mix together the yoghurt, curry powder, salt and black pepper and allow the escalopes to marinate in this mixture for 2 hours in the fridge. Barbecue the escalopes for 5 minutes, dipping them once or twice in the marinade whilst you cook them.

POULET À LA CITRONNELLE
(LEMONGRASS CHICKEN)
(8 servings)

Preparation time: 30 minutes
Cooking time: 55 minutes

3 drops of oil
1.5kg (3lb 5oz) chicken breasts, cut into this strips
2 small onions, finely chopped
3 fresh lemongrass stalks, finely chopped
1 pinch of chilli powder
2 tablespoons nuoc mam (Vietnamese fish sauce)
2 tablespoons soy sauce
Salt and black pepper
2 tablespoons sweetener

In a large pan (oiled and wiped with kitchen paper), brown the chicken, in batches if necessary, and sear it for 10 minutes. Add the onion, lemongrass, chilli powder, nuoc mam, soy sauce, salt, black pepper and sweetener. Lower the heat, cover and cook for 45 minutes.

POULET À L'INDIENNE
(MARINATED INDIAN CHICKEN)
(4 servings)

Preparation time: 40 minutes (plus 24 hours
    marinating)
Cooking time: 1 hour

450g (16oz) fat-free natural yoghurt
4 tablespoons chopped ginger
3 garlic cloves, chopped
1 teaspoon ground cinnamon
2 pinches of cayenne pepper
1 teaspoon coriander seeds
3 cloves
Grated zest of 1 lemon
10 mint leaves, chopped
1 whole chicken, cut into pieces
2 onions
Salt and black pepper
1 low-salt chicken stock cube

In a bowl, mix together the yoghurt, ginger, garlic, spices, lemon and mint leaves. Add the chicken pieces, seasoned with salt and pepper, and leave to marinate in the fridge for 24 hours. The following day, brown the onion in a non-stick casserole dish with 1 tablespoon water, then add the chicken and marinade sauce. Leave to simmer over a gentle heat for about 1 hour. Serve piping hot.

With the leftover juices, make up some soup using a low-salt chicken stock cube.

POULET AU GINGEMBRE
(GINGER CHICKEN)

(4 servings)

Preparation time: 20 minutes
Cooking time: 1 hour 10 minutes

3 drops of oil
2 large onions, finely chopped
3 garlic cloves, finely chopped
A few cloves
1 whole chicken, cut into pieces
5g (¼oz) piece of ginger, grated
Salt and black pepper

In a frying pan (oiled and wiped with kitchen paper), brown the onion and the garlic over a gentle heat. Stick cloves into the chicken pieces and add to the frying pan. Cover with water, add the ginger and season with salt and black pepper. Cook over a medium heat for at least an hour until all the water has evaporated.

POULET AU THYM
(THYME CHICKEN WITH A HERB SAUCE)

(4 servings)

Preparation time: 35 minutes
Cooking time: 35 minutes

You will need a steamer.

1 bunch of thyme
1 whole chicken, cut into pieces
Salt and black pepper
2 shallots, finely chopped
450g (16oz) fat-free natural yoghurt
Juice of ½ lemon
1 bunch of parsley, finely chopped
A few mint leaves, finely chopped
1 garlic clove, finely chopped

Pour a good quantity of water into the bottom part of the steamer, add salt and bring to the boil. In the upper part of the steamer, spread out half the thyme sprigs, place the chicken pieces on top of them and season. Cover with the rest of the thyme sprigs and the shallot. Put the lid on and as soon as steam starts to escape, cook for 30–35 minutes. In the meantime, pour the yoghurt into a dish, add the lemon juice, the parsley, mint leaves and garlic. Add salt and pepper, then mix all the ingredients together thoroughly and keep cool. Serve as an accompaniment for the chicken.

POULET AU YAOURT
(EASY CHICKEN CURRY)

(4 servings)

Preparation time: 15 minutes
Cooking time: 1 hour 30 minutes

1 whole chicken, cut into pieces and skin removed
125g (4½oz) onions, chopped
300g (10½oz) fat-free natural yoghurt
½ teaspoon ground ginger
½ teaspoon paprika
2 teaspoons lemon juice
2 teaspoons curry powder
Grated zest of ½ lemon
Salt and black pepper

Place the chicken pieces in a non-stick frying pan. Mix the other ingredients together, pour over the chicken and cover. Leave to simmer for about an hour and a half over a gentle heat. Season according to taste and, if necessary, remove the lid when the chicken is cooked to reduce the sauce. Serve piping hot.

POULET AUX CITRONS (CHICKEN WITH LEMONS)

(2 servings)

Preparation time: 15 minutes
Cooking time: 55 minutes

3 drops of oil
1 onion, finely chopped
2 garlic cloves, finely chopped
½ teaspoon finely chopped ginger
500g (1lb 2oz) chicken breast, cut into medium-sized cubes
Juice and zest of 2 lemons
2 tablespoons soy sauce
1 bouquet garni
1 pinch of cinnamon
1 pinch of ground ginger
Salt and black pepper

In a non-stick casserole dish (oiled and wiped with kitchen paper), brown the onion, garlic and ginger for 3–4 minutes over a medium heat. Add the chicken and sauté the pieces over a high heat for 2 minutes, stirring all the time with a spatula. Moisten with the juice of the 2 lemons, soy sauce and 150ml (5fl oz) water. Add the bouquet garni, cinnamon, ground ginger, lemon zest, salt and black pepper and leave to simmer, covered, over a gentle heat for 45 minutes. Serve piping hot.

POULET EXOTIQUE (CARDAMOM CHICKEN)

(4 servings)

Preparation time: 20 minutes
Cooking time: 1 hour 35 minutes

4 chicken legs
3 drops of oil
2 garlic cloves, finely chopped
2 onions, finely chopped
1 pinch of five-spice powder (star anise, cloves,
     pepper, cinnamon, fennel)
2 teaspoons curry powder
450g (16oz) fat-free natural yoghurt
1 cinnamon stick
2 teaspoons ground cumin
10 cardamom pods
1g (a good pinch) saffron threads
1 pinch of cayenne pepper

Remove the skin from the chicken legs and brown over a medium heat in a casserole dish (oiled and wiped with kitchen paper). Add the garlic and onion to the dish and brown for a few minutes. Beat the spice powder and curry powder into the yoghurt, then pour over the chicken. Cover and leave to cook over a gentle heat for 50 minutes. Add the cinnamon stick, cumin, cardamom, saffron and cayenne pepper. Continue cooking for 30 minutes. Place the chicken legs on a heated serving dish. Strain the sauce and mix in a blender for a few seconds so that it is completely smooth. Pour the sauce over the meat and serve immediately.

RILLETTES DE POULET (CHICKEN RILLETTES)

(3 servings)

Preparation time: 15 minutes (plus 2 hours
    refrigeration)
Cooking time: 5 minutes

3 drops of oil
500g (1lb 2oz) chicken breast (or turkey), cut into cubes
2 onions, roughly chopped
5 cornichons (small gherkins)
100g (3½oz) fat-free natural yoghurt
1 pinch of chilli powder
1 pinch of nutmeg
Salt and black pepper

In a frying pan (oiled and wiped with kitchen paper), brown the chicken over a high heat. Put the chicken pieces with all the other ingredients in a food processor (do not add too much salt) and blend until the texture is even. Pack the rillettes mixture into a terrine dish and keep refrigerated for at least 2 hours before serving.

SAUTÉ DE POULET AU CITRON ET AUX CÂPRES (SAUTÉED CHICKEN WITH LEMON AND CAPERS)

(4 servings)

Preparation time: 20 minutes
Cooking time: 20 minutes

3 drops of oil
1 red onion, finely chopped
800g (1lb 12oz) chicken breasts, cut into thin slices
Grated zest of 1 lemon
1 tablespoon small capers, drained and rinsed
75ml (2½fl oz) lemon juice
5 basil leaves, finely chopped
Salt and black pepper
In a non-stick frying pan (oiled and wiped with kitchen paper), pan-fry the onion until it turns golden brown, then put to one side. Brown the chicken slices in the same pan for 15 minutes over a medium heat. Add the onion, lemon zest, capers, lemon juice, basil, salt and black pepper. Serve piping hot.

TERRINE DE JAMBON
(CHICKEN AND PARSLEY TERRINE)

(8 servings)

Preparation time: 40 minutes (plus 2 hours 20 minutes
chilling time)
No cooking required

2 sachets of gelatine
1 large bunch of parsley, stalks removed and finely
chopped
200g (7oz) cooked chicken (or turkey), diced

Mix the 2 sachets of gelatine in 500ml (18fl oz) water
in a saucepan. Bring to the boil slowly, constantly
stirring. As soon as the first bubbles appear, remove
from the heat and leave to cool. Pour a thin layer of
gelatine into a cake tin and put it in the freezer for
3 minutes. Mix together the remaining gelatine with
the parsley and chicken. Pour half of this mixture into
the tin and freeze for 15 minutes. Add the rest of the
mixture to the tin and refrigerate for 2 hours. When
you want to turn the terrine out of the tin, place the
bottom of the tin into some hot water and turn upside
down to slide out.

SAUTÉ DE POULET AU PIMENT
(CHICKEN SAUTÉ WITH CHILLIES)

(4 servings)

Preparation time: 35 minutes
Cooking time: 15 minutes

4 chicken breasts
6 small red onions (or shallots)
3–6 red chillies
1 piece of ginger
1 fresh lemongrass stalk
4 garlic cloves
3 drops of oil
Salt and black pepper

Remove any skin from the chicken breasts and cut each one into eight pieces lengthways. Chop one onion into thin slices to garnish the dish. Finely blend the chillies, half the ginger and the lemongrass in a blender. Put to one side. In the blender, reduce the remaining onions, the garlic and the remaining half of the ginger to a purée. In a non-stick frying pan (oiled and wiped with kitchen paper), fry the chilli purée for 1–2 minutes. Add the chicken pieces, moving them around so that they are well covered with the chilli purée. Pour in 150ml (5fl oz) water and mix in the onion purée too. Add salt and pepper. Cook, uncovered, over a high heat for 5 minutes. Serve hot, garnished with the onion slices.

SOUFFLÉ DE FOIES DE VOLAILLE
(CHICKEN LIVER AND PARSLEY SOUFFLÉ)

(2 servings)

Preparation time: 20 minutes
Cooking time: 35 minutes

3 drops of oil
250g (9oz) chicken livers
1 garlic clove
1 bunch of parsley
4 eggs, separated
500ml (18fl oz) *Béchamel Sauce* (see page 375)
Salt and black pepper

Preheat the oven to 180°C/350°F/Gas 4.
In a non-stick frying pan (oiled and wiped with kitchen paper), brown the chicken livers, then chop them up with the garlic and parsley. Add the chopped liver mixture and the egg yolks to the *Béchamel Sauce* and mix together. Beat the egg whites and blend them into the mixture. Season well with pepper and salt. Place in the oven for 30 minutes, keeping a close eye on the colour of the soufflé. Serve immediately.

TERRINE DE FOIES DE VOLAILLE
(CHICKEN LIVER AND TARRAGON TERRINE)

(4 servings)

Preparation time: 15 minutes
Cooking time: 5 minutes

300g (10½oz) chicken livers
3 drops of oil
3 tablespoons raspberry vinegar
Salt and black pepper
1 bunch of tarragon
150g (5½oz) virtually fat-free fromage frais

Cook the chicken livers over a high heat in a non-stick frying pan (oiled and wiped with kitchen paper), and then deglaze the pan with the raspberry vinegar. Add salt and pepper. Pick off all the tarragon leaves and put them in a blender with the chicken livers and fromage frais. Purée the ingredients in a blender, then pour the mixture into a terrine dish. Refrigerate for 24 hours before serving.

COQUELET AU CITRON VERT EN CROÛTE DE SEL (LIME AND SALT-CRUSTED POUSSIN)

(2 servings)

Preparation time: 25 minutes (plus overnight
  marinating)
Cooking time: 50 minutes

1 bouquet garni
1½ limes
1 onion, chopped
1 poussin, weighing 400–500g (14oz–1lb 2oz)
2 egg whites
2kg (4½lb) coarse sea salt
Salt and black pepper

The day before, put the bouquet garni, juice of half
a lime, onion and poussin into 1 litre (1¾ pints) cold
water to marinate.

  Preheat the oven to 220°C/425°F/Gas 7.

  The following day, stuff the inside of the poussin
with the seasoning bits from the marinade. Mix the
egg whites with the cooking salt and cover the bottom
of a baking dish with this mixture. Place the poussin in
the middle of the dish and cover it with the remaining
salt. Bake the poussin in the oven for 50 minutes. To
serve, break the salt crust with the back of a spoon or a
hammer, brush away the salt and carefully remove the
skin. Halve the poussin and drizzle the remaining lime
juice over it to serve.

BLANCS DE DINDE EN PAQUETS
(TURKEY AND BRESAOLA PARCELS)

(4 servings)

Preparation time: 15 minutes
Cooking time: 30 minutes

4 x 100g (3½oz) turkey breasts
4 tablespoons mustard
4 slices of bresaola
Herbes de Provence (mixed herbs)
Salt and black pepper

Preheat the oven to 180°C/350°F/Gas 4.
If there is any fat, remove it from the turkey breasts, then place each one on an aluminium foil square. Coat each turkey breast with one tablespoonful of mustard, wrap a slice of bresaola around the breast and sprinkle it with the herbes de Provence. Add salt and black pepper. Sprinkle a little water over the meat, seal up the foil parcels and bake in the oven for 30 minutes.

DINDE AU LAIT
(NUTMEG AND MILK-BRAISED TURKEY)

(4 servings)

Preparation time: 20 minutes
Cooking time: 1 hour 5 minutes

1kg (2¼lb) whole boneless turkey joint
Salt and black pepper
1 pinch of nutmeg
5 garlic cloves, peeled
1 litre (1¾ pints) skimmed milk

Preheat the oven to 220°C/425°F/Gas 7.

Season the turkey with salt and pepper and grate a little nutmeg over the top. Place the turkey in a small but deep non-stick casserole dish along with the garlic cloves. Pour the milk over the turkey so that at least three-quarters of it is sitting in the milk. Gently heat the casserole dish for about 5 minutes on the top of the stove, then place in the oven and cook for 50 minutes or so, turning the bird over every 10 minutes. After 50 minutes, switch the oven off, cover the dish and leave it in there for another 10 minutes. Carve the turkey, remove the skin and serve with the carefully strained sauce.

ESCALOPES DE DINDE EN PAPILLOTES (PINK PEPPERCORN TURKEY ESCALOPES)

(4 servings)

Preparation time: 20 minutes
Cooking time: 25 minutes

4 small turkey breast steaks
100g (3½oz) virtually fat-free fromage frais
1 teaspoon cornflour
2 teaspoons wholegrain mustard
2 teaspoons Dijon mustard
Salt and black pepper
2 teaspoons pink peppercorns, ground
2 sprigs of thyme, chopped

Preheat the oven to 180°C/350°F/Gas 4.

Put each turkey breast on a sheet of clingfilm and bat into 1cm (½ inch) thick escalopes. Sear the escalopes in a non-stick frying pan or under the grill for 1 minute on each side. Put to one side on a plate. Beat together the fromage frais, cornflour and two mustards in a small bowl. Season with salt and black pepper, then add the pink peppercorns. Cut out four 20 x 30cm (8 x 12 inch) rectangles of greaseproof paper. Place an escalope onto each sheet, then divide the sauce among them. Sprinkle the thyme on top. Close up the parcels by folding the paper over itself several times. Place the parcels in a large dish and bake in the oven for about 25 minutes. Serve hot.

CAKE À LA DINDE
(TURKEY MEATLOAF)

(4 servings)

Preparation time: 15 minutes
Cooking time: 30 minutes

4 small turkey breast steaks (or chicken breasts),
   minced
1 large onion, finely chopped
2 tablespoons herbs and spices (cumin seeds, basil,
   herbes de Provence (mixed herbs), paprika, ginger)
Salt and black pepper
6 eggs
2 tablespoons cornflour

Preheat the oven to 180°C/350°F/Gas 4.
Mix the meat and onion together, add the spices,
herbs and salt and pepper, then blend in the eggs
and add the cornflour. Bake the mixture in a cake tin,
bain-marie or gratin dish for 20–30 minutes. Turn out
and slice to serve.

TIMBALES DE DINDE
(TURKEY TIMBALES)

(2 servings)

Preparation time: 30 minutes
Cooking time: 20 minutes

3 tablespoons virtually fat-free fromage frais
1 shallot, chopped
1 tablespoon parsley, finely chopped
½ garlic clove, crushed
1 lemon
Salt and black pepper
250g (9oz) turkey breast steak, cut into very thin strips

Preheat the oven to 180°C/350°F/Gas 4.
Mix together the fromage frais, shallot, parsley, garlic, a little lemon juice, salt and black pepper. In non-stick ramekin dishes, alternate layers of turkey strips with the herb mixture, finishing off with a layer of turkey. Place the dish into a bigger dish and fill this *bain-marie* half full with cold water. Cook for 20 minutes. Turn the timbales out of the ramekin dishes and serve hot.

Meat

BOEUF LUC LAC
(VIETNAMESE SHAKING BEEF)
(2 servings)

Preparation time: 10 minutes (plus 30 minutes
    marinating)
Cooking time: 5 minutes

400g (14oz) sirloin steak
2 tablespoons soy sauce
1 tablespoon oyster sauce
1 large piece of ginger, grated
Black pepper
3 drops of oil
4 garlic cloves, crushed
A few coriander leaves, chopped

Cut the beef into 1cm (½ inch) cubes. Mix with the
soy sauce, oyster sauce, ginger and black pepper.
Leave to marinate for at least 30 minutes. Just before
serving, brown the garlic in a frying pan (oiled and

wiped with kitchen paper). As soon as the garlic starts to brown and smell good, add the meat and cook it over a very high heat, stirring the mixture quickly, for 10–15 seconds. The meat should not be overcooked and should still be a little rare. Decorate with a few coriander leaves.

BOULETTES DE VIANDE AUX HERBES (MEATBALLS WITH ROSEMARY AND MINT)
(3 servings)

Preparation time: 30 minutes
Cooking time: 5 minutes per batch

1 medium onion, chopped
750g (1lb 10oz) minced beef
2 garlic cloves, crushed
1 egg, lightly beaten
2 tablespoons Chinese plum sauce
1 tablespoon Worcestershire sauce
2 tablespoons finely chopped rosemary
1–2 tablespoons finely chopped mint or basil
Salt and black pepper

Mix together the onion, minced meat, garlic, egg, plum and Worcestershire sauces and the herbs. Add salt and pepper and shape into meatballs the size of a walnut. Cook the meatballs, a few at a time, in a saucepan over a medium heat for about 5 minutes until they are golden brown on all sides. Allow any fat to drain off onto kitchen paper.

BOULETTES ORIENTALES (ASIAN MEATBALLS)

(3 servings)

Preparation time: 20 minutes
Cooking time: 20 minutes

500g (1lb 2oz) lean minced veal
3 tablespoons soy sauce
2 tablespoons sherry vinegar
½ low-salt beef stock cube
2 large garlic cloves, finely chopped
½ teaspoon grated ginger
2 shallots, cut into tiny pieces
Salt and black pepper
1 teaspoon cornflour

Shape the veal into small meatballs. Brown the meatballs on all sides in a large non-stick frying pan, over a high heat, for 7 minutes, then put them to one side. Pour a cup of water into the pan and mix it thoroughly with the meat juices. Add all the other ingredients except the cornflour. Mix well and return the meatballs to the pan, pouring in just enough water so that the meatballs sit in the sauce, but are not completely covered. Cook over a medium heat for 10 minutes until the meatballs are cooked right through. Blend the cornflour with a little cold water and add to the sauce to thicken it to taste.

FOIE DE VEAU AU VINAIGRE DE FRAMBOISE (CALF'S LIVER WITH RASPBERRY VINEGAR)

(1 serving)

Preparation time: 15 minutes
Cooking time: 15 minutes

3 drops of oil
1 small onion, thinly sliced
100g (3½oz) calf's liver, sliced
Salt and black pepper
1 shallot, finely chopped
1 tablespoon raspberry vinegar
1 teaspoon thyme
½ bay leaf

In a non-stick frying pan (oiled and wiped with kitchen paper), fry the onion slices over a medium heat. As soon as they turn golden brown, put them to one side on a plate. Place the slices of calf's liver in the oiled frying pan and lightly fry for about 4 minutes on each side. Season with salt and pepper and put to one side, covering them so that they keep hot. In the same pan, cook the shallot over a medium heat until it is soft. Add the raspberry vinegar, thyme and bay leaf and cook for 2 minutes, stirring all the time, then put the liver back in the frying pan and heat it through again in this mixture. Serve immediately.

ROULADES DE JAMBON (HAM ROULADES)

(4 servings)

Preparation time: 10 minutes (plus 30 minutes chilling)
No cooking required

1 garlic clove, finely chopped
½ bunch of chives, chopped
200g (7oz) virtually fat-free quark
8 slices of extra-lean ham
8 lettuce leaves
4 sprigs of parsley

Mix the garlic and chives into the quark. Spread the quark mixture over the slices of ham and roll them up. Put in the fridge for 30 minutes for the quark mixture to set. Decorate each plate with 2 lettuce leaves, then place a couple of ham roulades onto this bed of salad. To garnish, add a sprig of parsley.

AMUSE-GUEULE AU JAMBON
(LITTLE HAM APPETIZERS)

(4 servings)

Preparation time: 10 minutes
No cooking required

175g (6oz) extra-lean ham, chopped
225g (8oz) virtually fat-free quark
A few chives, finely chopped
4 shallots, finely chopped
Marjoram (or another herb, depending on your taste),
    finely chopped
A few drops of Tabasco

Mix all the ingredients together thoroughly. Roll the mixture into tiny balls and place on a nice serving dish.

PÂTÉ DE CAMPAGNE (COUNTRY PÂTÉ)

(8 servings)

Preparation time: 20 minutes
Cooking time: 1 hour

12 slices of cooked turkey
200g (7oz) chicken livers
250g (9oz) extra-lean ham
1 onion
700g (1lb 9oz) minced beef (5% fat)

4 cloves
4 garlic cloves, crushed
1 tablespoon red port, boiled
1 pinch of nutmeg
1 teaspoon thyme
1 teaspoon oregano
Pepper

Preheat the oven to 200°C/ 400°F/Gas 6.

Blend in a food processor or finely chop 4 slices of the turkey, the livers, ham and onion. Turn out into a bowl and add the minced meat. Grind the cloves with a pestle and mortar, then add the garlic, port, nutmeg, herbs and some pepper and mix everything together. Line the tin with the remaining turkey slices so that they generously overlap the sides of the container. Press the mixture into the tin firmly, then tap the tin on the table to get rid of any air bubbles. Fold the turkey over the top, cover and bake for 1 hour. Allow to settle for 5 minutes, then drain off any surplus liquid and leave to cool before serving.

LAPIN EN PAPILLOTE
(RABBIT AND CHICKEN HERB PARCELS)

(2 servings)

Preparation time: 15 minutes
Cooking time: 1 hour

2 chicken breasts
3 drops of oil
2 saddles of rabbit
A mixture of thyme, bay leaves, savory, marjoram or
 rosemary
Salt and black pepper

Preheat the oven to 220°C/425°F/Gas 7.

Put each chicken breast on a sheet of clingfilm and bat into very thin escalopes. In a non-stick frying pan (oiled and wiped with kitchen paper), quickly cook the chicken escalopes over a very high heat. Cut each saddle into two pieces and place half a chicken escalope around each piece. Place each saddle onto some aluminium foil and add the herbs. Season according to taste. Make the foil into parcels and bake for 50 minutes.

LAPIN SAUCE PIQUANTE
(RABBIT IN A MUSTARD AND CAPERS SAUCE)
(4 servings)

Preparation time: 30 minutes
Cooking time: 1 hour 15 minutes

3 drops of oil
1 rabbit, cut into pieces
1 shallot, finely chopped
Salt and black pepper
8 teaspoons virtually fat-free fromage frais
1 tablespoon mustard
1 tablespoon capers
A few cornichons (small gherkins), cut into slices

In a casserole dish (oiled and wiped with kitchen paper), brown the rabbit with the shallot. Add salt and pepper and cook gently, uncovered, for about an hour. Now, mix in the fromage frais, mustard, capers and cornichons. Heat it all through for a few minutes, being careful not to allow the sauce to boil, then serve.

Eggs

BROUILLADE AU SAUMON FUMÉ
(SMOKED SALMON WITH SCRAMBLED EGGS)

4 servings

Preparation time: 10 minutes
Cooking time: 10 minutes

8 eggs
Salt and black pepper
100g (3½ oz) smoked salmon, cut into thin strips
75ml (2½fl oz) skimmed milk
1 tablespoon virtually fat-free fromage frais
4 chives, chopped

Beat the eggs together in a bowl and season sparingly with salt and pepper. Heat a saucepan with a little skimmed milk in the bottom. Pour in the eggs and cook over a gentle heat, stirring all the time with a spatula. Remove from the heat and stir in the salmon and fromage frais. Serve immediately, decorated with a few chives.

ŒUFS BROUILLÉS
(SCRAMBLED EGGS WITH HERBS)

(2 servings)

Preparation time: 10 minutes
Cooking time: 10 minutes

4 eggs
125ml (4fl oz) skimmed milk
Salt and black pepper
1 pinch of nutmeg
2 sprigs of parsley (or chives), chopped

Beat the eggs together thoroughly in a glass bowl, add the milk, and then season with salt and pepper. Grate in a little nutmeg and cook gently in a *bain-marie* or by placing the bowl over a pan of simmering water, stirring continuously. Serve immediately, sprinkled with the chopped parsley or chives.

OEUFS BROUILLÉS AU CRABE
(SCRAMBLED EGGS WITH CRAB)

(4 servings)

Preparation time: 10 minutes
Cooking time: 10 minutes

6 medium eggs
2 tablespoons nuoc mam (Vietnamese fish sauce)
2 medium shallots, finely chopped
3 drops of oil
100g (3½oz) white crab meat, well drained

Lightly beat together the eggs and the fish sauce in a bowl. Cook the shallot for 1 minute in a non-stick frying pan (oiled and wiped with kitchen paper) until it turns golden and add to the eggs. Fry the crab meat until it is slightly browned and stir this into the eggs. Heat this mixture for 3–5 minutes over a moderate heat until it has scrambled without turning brown. Remove from the heat and serve immediately.

OEUFS COCOTTE AU SAUMON
(SALMON EGGS COCOTTE)
(6 servings)

Preparation time: 10 minutes
Cooking time: 5 minutes

12 teaspoons virtually fat-free fromage frais
Tarragon (or chervil), chopped
2 nice slices of smoked salmon
6 eggs
Salt and black pepper

Put 2 teaspoons fromage frais and a pinch of herbs into six ramekin dishes. To this, add a third of a slice of smoked salmon, cut into very fine strips, then one egg and some salt and pepper. Place the ramekin dishes in a high-sided saucepan filled with boiling water like a bain-marie. Cover and cook for 3–5 minutes over a medium heat.

Instead of salmon you may use ham, bresaola or any other protein that suits your taste.

ŒUFS DURS AU CURRY
(CURRIED HARD-BOILED EGGS)

(1 serving)

Preparation time: 10 minutes
Cooking time: 25 minutes

2 eggs
½ onion, chopped
8 tablespoons skimmed milk
1 pinch of cornflour
Salt and black pepper
1 teaspoon curry powder

Cook the eggs for 10 minutes in boiling water until hard-boiled. Meanwhile, cook the onion in a saucepan over a medium heat with half the milk for 10 minutes, stirring continuously. Add the cornflour blended with the rest of the cold milk and stir vigorously. Add the salt, pepper and curry powder. Slice the eggs and arrange in a dish. Pour the sauce over the eggs to serve.

ŒUFS FARCIS AUX MAQUEREAUX
(EGGS STUFFED WITH MACKEREL)

(4 servings)

Preparation time: 15 minutes
Cooking time: 10 minutes

4 eggs
1 tin of mackerel fillets in white wine, well drained
15g (½oz) virtually fat-free quark
15g (½oz) virtually fat-free fromage frais
Mustard
Salt and black pepper

Cook the eggs for 10 minutes in boiling water until hard-boiled. Cut the eggs in two lengthways. Put the yolks in a bowl and keep the whites for later. Add the mackerel fillets, quark, fromage frais, mustard, salt and pepper to the bowl. Crush and mix everything together with a fork. Using a large spoon, divide the mixture evenly into the egg white halves to make them into 'whole eggs' again. Put in a cool place before eating them.

OMELETTE AU THON (TUNA OMELETTE)

(4 servings)

Preparation time: 10 minutes
Cooking time: 5 minutes

8 eggs
2 anchovy fillets, cut into tiny strips
200g (7oz) tuna, in brine or spring water, flaked
1 tablespoon chopped parsley
Black pepper
3 drops of oil

Beat the eggs together and add the anchovy and tuna to them. Season with the parsley and pepper. Cook the omelette over a medium heat in a non-stick frying pan (oiled and wiped with kitchen paper). Serve immediately.

PETITS FLANS AU CRABE
(LITTLE CRAB FLANS)

(5 servings)

Preparation time: 10 minutes
Cooking time: 45 minutes

200g (7oz) smoked salmon, diced
2 eggs
1 tablespoon cornflour
350ml (12fl oz) milk
1 small tin of white crab meat, well drained
Salt and black pepper
¼ teaspoon fish stock

Preheat the oven to 180°C/350°F/Gas 4.
Divide the smoked salmon among five ramekin dishes. Beat together the eggs and the cornflour blended with the cold milk, then add the crab. Season with salt and pepper and add the fish stock. Pour the mixture into the ramekins. Place the ramekins into a bigger dish and fill this *bain-marie* half full with cold water. Bake for 45 minutes.

QUICHE (NO-PASTRY CHICKEN QUICHE)

(2 servings)

Preparation time: 15 minutes
Cooking time: 20 minutes

6 tablespoons virtually fat-free fromage frais
3 eggs, beaten
2 slices of cooked chicken, cut into small pieces
½ onion, chopped
1 pinch of nutmeg
Salt and black pepper
3 drops of oil

Preheat the oven to 240°C/475 °F/ Gas 9.
Mix together all the ingredients except the oil. Put the mixture in a flan dish (oiled and wiped with kitchen paper) and bake for 20 minutes.

SOUFFLÉ AU JAMBON (HAM SOUFFLÉ)

(4 servings)

Preparation time: 15 minutes
Cooking time: 45 minutes

200ml (7fl oz) skimmed milk
20g (¾oz) cornflour
4 eggs, separated
400g (14oz) virtually fat-free fromage frais
200g (7oz) extra-lean ham, cut into strips
1 pinch of nutmeg
Salt and black pepper

Preheat the oven to 220°C/425°F/Gas 7.
Blend together the cold milk and cornflour. Beat the egg yolks with the fromage frais and pour over the milk, stirring all the time to obtain a smooth paste. Add the ham and nutmeg and season with salt and pepper. Beat the egg whites until very stiff and carefully blend them into the ham mixture. Pour the mixture into a non-stick soufflé tin and adjust the seasoning. Bake in the oven for 45 minutes.

TERRINE D'ŒUFS AU SAUMON
(SALMON AND EGG TERRINE)

(8 to 10 servings)

Preparation time: 30 minutes (plus overnight setting)
Cooking time: 10 minutes

Prepare this recipe the day before you wish to eat the
terrine.

10 eggs
2 large handfuls of chopped herbs (parsley, chives,
tarragon)
4 thick slices of smoked salmon
300g (10½oz) gelatine (prepared from a sachet)
Dukan Mayonnaise (see page 358)

Cook the eggs for 10 minutes in boiling water until
hard-boiled. Leave them to cool, then chop them
up with a knife and mix with half the herbs. Arrange
the eggs in a terrine dish, alternating them with the
salmon slices. Melt the gelatine and pour it over the
eggs. Leave to set for 24 hours in the fridge. Add the
rest of the herbs to the mayonnaise. Serve the terrine
cut into slices with the herb mayonnaise.

Seafood and Fish

GÂTEAU DE CREVETTES
(BAKED PRAWN FRITTATA)

(2 servings)

Preparation time: 10 minutes
Cooking time: 30 minutes

4 eggs
Salt and black pepper
500g (1lb 2oz) virtually fat-free fromage frais
300g (10½oz) shelled prawns

Preheat the oven to 200°C/400°F/Gas 6.
Beat the eggs with the seasoning and then gradually work in the fromage frais, stirring thoroughly. Add the prawns. Put the mixture into a baking dish and cook for 30 minutes.

TARTARE DE CREVETTES (PRAWN TARTARE)

(2 servings)

Preparation time: 10 minutes
No cooking required

5 sprigs of dill, very finely chopped
6 tablespoons *Dukan Mayonnaise* (see page 358)
250g (9oz) cooked prawns, shelled, roughly chopped
2 pinches of paprika
Black pepper

Stir the dill into the mayonnaise and add the prawns.
Sprinkle over the paprika. Stir the mixture once again,
then add the black pepper.

MOUSSE DE SAINT-JACQUES (SCALLOP MOUSSE)

(4 servings)

Preparation time: 15 minutes
Cooking time: 15 minutes

You will need a large steamer.

8 scallops, out of shell
200g (7oz) virtually fat-free fromage frais
2 eggs, separated
Salt and black pepper

Mix the scallops with the fromage frais, add the egg yolks, then season. Gently fold in the stiffly beaten egg whites. Put this mixture into four ramekin dishes and steam for 15 minutes in a big steamer. Turn out the mousses and serve hot, perhaps with the *Sauce Citron* (see page 368).

OMELETTE AUX FRUITS DE MER (SEAFOOD OMELETTE)

(2 servings)

Preparation time: 20 minutes
Cooking time: 30 minutes

2 eggs
250ml (9fl oz) skimmed milk
1 small tin of white crab meat
A big handful of shelled cooked prawns
A big handful of cooked mussels
Salt and black pepper

Preheat the oven to 220°C/425°F/Gas 7.
Beat the eggs and milk together in a bowl. Drain the crab and add to the bowl with the prawns and mussels. Mix thoroughly and season. Pour the mixture into two ramekin dishes. Place the dishes into a bigger dish and fill this bain-marie half full with cold water. Bake for 30 minutes.

TERRINE AUX FRUITS DE MER
(SEAFOOD TERRINE)

(2 servings)

Preparation time: 15 minutes
Cooking time: 30 minutes

4 tablespoons oat bran
3 tablespoons virtually fat-free fromage frais
3 eggs
1 generous handful of mixed seafood (fresh or frozen)
Salt and black pepper
Herbs of your choice

Preheat the oven to 180°C/350°F/Gas 4.
Mix all the ingredients together until the mixture is smooth. Put the mixture into a greaseproof-lined cake tin and bake for 30 minutes.

AILE DE RAIE AUX FINES HERBES
(SKATE WING WITH AROMATIC HERBS)

(2 servings)

Preparation time: 25 minutes
Cooking time: 5 minutes

You will need a pressure cooker.

1 quite thick skate wing, skin on
1 large bunch of different herbs (chives, parsley,
    tarragon etc)
Salt and black pepper
75ml (2½fl oz) vinegar
1 lemon (½ for the juice, the other ½ to garnish)

Wash the skate wing thoroughly. Place it on a bed of aromatic herbs (leaving a few for sprinkling over and the garnish) in the perforated steamer basket of the pressure cooker. Add salt and pepper and sprinkle a few herbs over the fish. Pour two glasses of vinegar water into the pressure cooker and place the steamer basket in the high position. Seal the pressure cooker and cook for 5 minutes once pressure has been reached. When the fish is cooked, remove the skin and herbs. Separate the upper part of the wing from the bone and place the fish onto a hot plate. Do the same for the lower part of the wing. Season the fish with salt and pepper, squeeze the lemon juice over it, sprinkle 1 tablespoon chopped herbs on top and serve nice and hot, garnished with lemon wedges.

RAIE SAUCE BLANCHE
(SKATE IN A CREAMY TARRAGON SAUCE)

(2 servings)

Preparation time: 20 minutes
Cooking time: 20 minutes

2 skate wings, skin on
A splash of vinegar
3 bay leaves
1 shallot, chopped
2 tablespoons tarragon vinegar
Salt and black pepper
30g (1oz) capers
100g (3½oz) virtually fat-free fromage frais

Poach the skate wings with a splash of vinegar and the bay leaves in 750ml (1¼ pints) simmering water for 8–10 minutes. In the meantime, over a medium heat gently fry the shallot with the tarragon vinegar, salt and pepper. When the shallot seems slightly caramelized, turn the heat right down and add the capers and fromage frais, stirring slowly so that you avoid overheating the sauce. Remove any skin from the skate and serve it covered with the white sauce.

CABILLAUD SAUCE MOUTARDE
(COD WITH MUSTARD SAUCE)

(1 serving)

Preparation time: 10 minutes
Cooking time: 15 minutes

You will need a steamer.

1 nice cod fillet
Salt and black pepper
150g (5½oz) fat-free natural yoghurt
1 tablespoon mustard
Lemon juice (to taste)
2 tablespoons capers
1 bunch of parsley, finely chopped

Sprinkle some salt over the cod fillet and steam for 8–10 minutes (depending on its thickness). In the meantime, put the yoghurt, mustard, some lemon juice, capers, parsley and black pepper into a saucepan. Warm over a gentle heat. Place the cooked fish into a serving dish, pour the sauce over it and serve nice and hot.

FILET DE CABILLAUD AUX ÉCHALOTES ET À LA MOUTARDE (COD WITH SHALLOTS AND MUSTARD)

(2 servings)

Preparation time: 20 minutes
Cooking time: 25 minutes

4 shallots, chopped
50g (1¾oz) virtually fat-free fromage frais
1 tablespoon mustard
2 tablespoons lemon juice
Salt and black pepper
400g (14oz) cod fillet

Preheat the oven to 180°C/350°F/Gas 4.
Put the shallot in a saucepan with 1 tablespoon water and reduce until it turns translucent. Mix together the fromage frais with the mustard and lemon juice and season. Place the shallot reduction in the bottom of a baking dish. Place the cod on top and pour the fromage frais sauce over the fish. Bake in the oven for about 15 minutes.

FILET DE LIEU À L'INDIENNE
(SPICY INDIAN POLLOCK)

(2 servings)

Preparation time: 20 minutes
Cooking time: 20 minutes

300g (10½oz) pollock or coley fillet
250ml (9fl oz) court bouillon or stock
1 medium onion, chopped
3 drops of oil
1 egg yolk
Salt and black pepper
½ teaspoon curry powder
1 pinch of saffron
1 tablespoon chopped parsley

Poach the fish fillets in the hot court bouillon for about 5 minutes. In the meantime, brown the onion in a non-stick frying pan (oiled and wiped with kitchen paper). Moisten with a cup of the court bouillon and reduce for 2 minutes. Add the egg yolk, diluted in a little of the liquid, and allow the sauce to gradually thicken. Season, then add the curry powder and saffron. Arrange the fish fillets in a hot serving dish and pour the sauce over them, sprinkling with the chopped parsley to garnish.

LIEU AUX CÂPRES
(POLLOCK WITH A CREAMY CAPER SAUCE)

(2 servings)

Preparation time: 25 minutes
Cooking time: 15 minutes

4 slices of pollock fillet
1 bay leaf
3 peppercorns
Salt
150g (5½oz) fat-free natural yoghurt
1 egg yolk
2 tablespoons lemon juice
2 tablespoons capers
1 tablespoon flat-leaf parsley, finely chopped
1 tablespoon chives, finely chopped

Place the pollock slices in a large non-stick, high-sided frying pan. Add the bay leaf, peppercorns and salt. Cover with cold water. Warm over a low heat and leave to simmer for 10 minutes. Pour the yoghurt into a small saucepan and heat gently. In a bowl, mix together the egg yolk and lemon juice, then pour into the saucepan, stirring vigorously until the sauce starts to simmer. Add the capers, parsley and chives. Drain the fish and arrange it on a serving dish with the sauce poured over it.

TERRINE DE MERLAN (WHITING TERRINE)

(2 servings)

Preparation time: 20 minutes
Cooking time: 20 minutes

600g (1¼lb) whiting
2 litres (3½ pints) court bouillon or stock
1 egg
2 tablespoons virtually fat-free fromage frais
Salt and black pepper
Herbs (basil, tarragon, coriander)

Preheat the oven to 180°C/350°F/Gas 4.
Cook the whiting in the court bouillon. Whiz it in a blender and mix it with the beaten egg and fromage frais. Season with salt and pepper, then add the herbs. Put this mixture into two ramekin dishes. Place these dishes into a bigger dish and fill this *bain-marie* half full with cold water. Bake for 20 minutes.

ESCALOPES DE SAUMON RÔTIES
À LA SAUCE MOUTARDE
(SALMON ESCALOPES IN A MUSTARD DILL SAUCE)

(4 servings)

Preparation time: 20 minutes
Cooking time: 15 minutes

4 thick pieces of salmon, weighing 200g (7oz) each
2 shallots, chopped
1 tablespoon mild mustard
6 teaspoons virtually fat-free fromage frais
Finely chopped dill
Salt and black pepper

Put the salmon in the freezer for a few minutes so that you can cut it into thin 50g (1¾oz) slices. Gently fry the salmon slices in a non-stick frying pan for 1 minute on each side over a medium heat. Remove and keep warm. Brown the shallot in the same frying pan, cover with the mustard and fromage frais and allow to thicken for 5 minutes over a gentle heat. Return the salmon to the frying pan with some dill, salt and pepper for a few seconds, then serve immediately.

COEUR DE SAUMON
(SALMON HEART FRITTATA)

(3 servings)

Preparation time: 10 minutes
Cooking time: 45 minutes

10g (¼oz) cornflour
425g (15oz) hake fillet, flaked
3 eggs, beaten
100g (3½oz) virtually fat-free fromage frais
Salt and black pepper
100ml (3½fl oz) water
140g (5oz) salmon fillet

Preheat the oven to 220°C/425°F/Gas 7.
Blend the cornflour with a little cold water. Mix together the hake, eggs, fromage frais, cornflour and salt and pepper. Pour into a 22cm (9 inch) wide cake tin. Place the salmon fillet in the middle of the mixture and bake in the oven for 45 minutes.

ROULÉ AU SAUMON FUMÉ
(SMOKED SALMON ROULÉ)

(3 servings)

Preparation time: 10 minutes (plus 3 hours chilling
   time)
Cooking time: 15 minutes

3 eggs
3 teaspoons cornflour
3 drops of oil
250g (9oz) virtually fat-free fromage frais
2 tablespoons chopped chives
1 tablespoon chopped ginger
100g (3½oz) smoked salmon, chopped
Black pepper
A few sprigs of parsley

Mix together 1 egg, 1 tablespoon water, 1 teaspoon
of the cornflour and use this to make a thin omelette
in a non-stick frying pan (oiled and wiped with kitchen
paper). Repeat this with the rest of the eggs, water
and cornflour. Spread the fromage frais carefully over
each omelette, sprinkle over the chives and ginger,
divide out the salmon equally and add pepper. Roll
up each omelette very tightly in clingfilm. Refrigerate
for 3 hours. Using a very sharp knife, cut the rolls into
slices and serve on a dish decorated with the parsley.

SAUMON FARCI
(HERB-STUFFED BAKED SALMON)

(6 servings)

Preparation time: 30 minutes (plus 2 hours marinating)
Cooking time: 40 minutes

1 bunch of flat-leaf parsley, chopped
1 bunch of coriander, chopped
½ chilli, chopped
5 fresh lemongrass stalks, chopped
2 handfuls of shallots, chopped
4 garlic cloves, chopped
1 lemon, cut into very thin slices
1 teaspoon ground cumin
1 teaspoon grated ginger
100ml (3½fl oz) white wine
Salt and black pepper
1 salmon, weighing around 1.5kg (3lb 5oz) without the
    central bone
2 eggs

Preheat the oven to 200°C/400°F/Gas 6.

Mix all the ingredients except the salmon and eggs a in a bowl and leave the salmon to marinate for a few hours in a cool place. Open up the salmon and season it with salt and pepper. Stuff the inside of the fish with the marinade. Place the salmon on a sheet of greaseproof paper and bake for 40 minutes.

SAUMON FUMÉ AU PETIT SUISSE (SMOKED SALMON APPETIZERS)

(2 servings)

Preparation time: 5 minutes
No cooking required

You will need chives or wooden cocktail sticks.

300g (10½ oz) virtually fat-free fromage frais
60g (2¼oz) virtually fat-free quark
1 small jar of salmon roe
Salt and black pepper
4 slices of smoked salmon

Beat together the fromage frais and quark. Carefully fold in the salmon roe, salt and pepper. Place a little of this mixture onto each slice of salmon. Roll up the slices and keep them in place either with a chive or a wooden cocktail stick. Keep refrigerated until you want to serve them. Decorate with a few salmon roe scattered on top. Eat with some mini Dukan galettes.

TERRINE DE SAUMON ET LOTTE AU CITRON VERT (SALMON AND MONKFISH TERRINE WITH LIME)

(2–3 servings)

Preparation time: 30 minutes (plus 1 hour marinating and 4 hours setting time)
No cooking required

400g (14oz) fresh salmon fillet
200g (7oz) monkfish fillet, completely skinned
100ml (3½fl oz) lime juice
A hint of Tabasco
1 pinch of nutmeg
Black pepper
2 sachets of gelatine
1 teaspoon pink peppercorns
4 small white onions, chopped
2 large sprigs of basil, finely chopped

Cut the fish into very thin slices and place them in a shallow dish. Mix together the lime, Tabasco, nutmeg and pepper. Pour this over the fish and leave to marinate for 1 hour in the fridge. In the meantime, prepare the gelatine according to the instructions, using 500ml (18fl oz) water for both sachets. Allow to cool to room temperature. Drain the fish. Use clingfilm to line a cake tin that holds at least 1 litre (1¾ pints). The clingfilm should generously overlap the tin. Pour a thin layer of the gelatine into the bottom of the tin and let it set in the fridge. Then arrange alternate layers of monkfish and salmon, scattering over the layers the barely crushed pink peppercorns, onion and basil. Pour in the remaining gelatine. Shake the tin a little so that the gelatine gets right down to the bottom and does not leave any gaps. Fold the clingfilm over the top to completely cover the tin and leave to set in the fridge for at least 4 hours.

DORADE RAFFINÉE
(SEA BREAM WITH SAFFRON)

(1 serving)

Preparation time: 15 minutes
Cooking time: 10 minutes

150g (5½oz) sea bream fillet
Salt and black pepper
1 saffron thread
150g (5½oz) virtually fat-free fromage frais

Preheat the oven to 220°C/425°F/Gas 7.
Place the sea bream fillet in a baking dish. Season with salt and pepper. Mix the saffron thread into the fromage frais and spread this over the fillet. Cover with a sheet of aluminium foil. Bake for about 10 minutes.

TARTARE DE DORADE ÉPICÉE
(SPICY SEA BREAM TARTARE)

(6 servings)

Preparation time: 15 minutes
No cooking required

1.2kg (2½lb) sea bream fillet
Juice of 2 lemons
3 shallots, chopped
1 cucumber
1 bunch of herbs (flat-leaf parsley, dill, chervil, chives),
   chopped
Salt and black pepper
A few drops of Tabasco

Roughly chop up the fish in a blender. Peel the cucumber and cut into small pieces. Mix the fish, lemon juice, shallot, cucumber and herbs together in a large bowl and season with salt, pepper and Tabasco.

DORADE EN CROÛTE DE SEL
(SALT-CRUSTED SEA BREAM)

(4 servings)

Preparation time: 10 minutes
Cooking time: 1 hour 30 minutes

1 whole sea bream, weighing 1–1.5kg (2¼–3lb 5oz),
   cleaned, but do not remove the scales
5kg (11lb) coarse sea salt

Preheat the oven to 230°C/450°F/Gas 8.
Select a casserole dish slightly larger than the fish. Line the bottom and sides with aluminium foil. Fill the bottom of the casserole dish with a layer of salt 3cm (1¼ inch) thick. Place the sea bream on top of the salt and cover it with the remaining salt. The fish should be completely covered. Sprinkle with a little water to form the crust. Cook for 1 hour, then lower the temperature to 180°C/350°F/Gas 4 and continue cooking for 30 minutes. Turn the contents of the casserole dish out onto a chopping board, then extract the fish by breaking the salt crust with the back of a spoon or a hammer. Brush away the salt and carefully remove the skin before serving.

DORADE EN PAPILLOTE À LA COMPOTE D'OIGNONS (BAKED SEA BREAM WITH ONION COMPOTE)

(2 servings)

Preparation time: 20 minutes
Cooking time: 15 minutes

1 large onion, chopped
3 drops of oil
2 sea bream fillets
Salt and black pepper
1 tablespoon parsley, chopped

Preheat the oven to 180°C/350°F/Gas 4.

Fry the onion gently in a non-stick frying pan (oiled and wiped with kitchen paper) over a gentle heat. The onion must not brown. Spread the onion out over two sheets of greaseproof paper, and then place a sea bream fillet on top. Add salt and pepper and sprinkle with the parsley. Seal the parcels carefully and place them in a baking dish. Bake for about 15 minutes.

POISSON AU OVEN
(BAKED FISH WITH HERBS)

(4 servings)

Preparation time: 15 minutes
Cooking time: 55 minutes

800g (1¾lb) fish fillets (sea bream, cod, pollock or
    coley)
Salt and black pepper
300g (10½oz) virtually fat-free fromage frais
4 eggs
5 tablespoons chopped herbs (parsley, tarragon,
    chives)
3 drops of oil

Preheat the oven to 220°C/425°F/Gas 7.
Place the fish fillets into greaseproof paper parcels
with some salt and pepper and bake for 10 minutes.
Turn the oven temperature down to 180°C/350°F/Gas
4. Put the cooked fillets into a blender along with the
fromage frais, eggs and herbs and blend everything
together. Pour the mixture into a baking dish (oiled
and wiped with kitchen paper). Place the dish into a
bigger dish and fill this *bain-marie* half full with cold
water. Bake for about 45 minutes.

TARTARE DE LOUP AUX CITRONS VERTS
(SEA BASS TARTARE WITH LIME)

(2 servings)

Preparation time: 20 minutes
No cooking required

400g (14 oz) sea bass fillet
2 shallots, finely chopped
4 limes, sliced
125g (4½oz) virtually fat-free fromage frais
Salt and black pepper
Juice of ½ lemon
A few chives, finely chopped

With a knife, cut the fish up roughly into small pieces and mix with the shallot. Arrange on plates garnished with the lime slices. Lightly beat the fromage frais, season, and add the lemon juice. Pour this over the tartare and serve cold, garnished with the chives.

FILET DE BAR À LA VAPEUR DE MENTHE CANNELLE (MINT AND CINNAMON-SCENTED SEA BASS)

(4 servings)

Preparation time: 10 minutes
Cooking time: 10 minutes

½ teaspoon ground cinnamon
3 sprigs of mint
4 sea bass fillets, with the skin on
Salt and black pepper
½ lemon
2 cinnamon sticks

Put some water in the bottom of a steamer along with the ground cinnamon and mint, putting aside a few leaves for garnish, and heat. Place the fish fillets in the upper part of the steamer and cook for 10 minutes, then season with salt and black pepper. Serve the fish, squeezing a trickle of lemon juice over it and decorating with the mint leaves and half a cinnamon stick.

MAQUEREAUX À LA BRETONNE
(BRETON-STYLE MACKEREL)

(3 servings)

Preparation time: 30 minutes
Cooking time: 30 minutes

6 mackerel
3 shallots, chopped
1 small bunch of parsley, chopped
2 tablespoons chives, chopped
6 tablespoons cider vinegar

Preheat the oven to 200°C/400°F/Gas 6.

Gut the fish through the gills and clean out the insides, remembering to remove the small black membrane. Wash the fish and cut off the fins and tails. Cut out six sheets of thick aluminium foil and place the fish on top of them. Stuff the fish with the shallot and chopped herbs and add a tablespoon of vinegar to each parcel. Seal the parcels carefully and grill on the barbecue or bake in the oven for about 30 minutes.

RILLETTES DE MAQUEREAUX
(MACKEREL RILLETTES)

(4 servings)

Preparation time: 20 minutes
Cooking time: 20 minutes

2 litres (3½ pints) court bouillon or fish stock
1kg (2¼lb) mackerel
Coarse sea salt
5 tablespoons tarragon or green peppercorn mustard
2 lemons
Parsley (or chives), finely chopped

Prepare your court bouillon or stock well in advance to allow it time to cool. Gut the fish through the gills and clean out the insides, remembering to remove the small black membrane. Wash the fish and cut off the fins and tails. Put the mackerel in the cold court bouillon that has been salted with the coarse sea salt. Warm over a high heat and, as soon as the liquid starts to boil, turn off the heat, cover and leave for 5 minutes. Take the mackerel out and let them cool. Using a knife, take off the skin and remove the meat from each mackerel, then crush the mackerel with a fork. Mix the mackerel with the mustard that has been diluted with the juice from the two lemons along with either the parsley or chives. Press the mackerel mixture into little stoneware pots and decorate with small lemon wedges and sprigs of parsley.

TARTARE DE THON
(TUNA TARTARE)

(4 servings)

Preparation time: 15 minutes (plus 15 minutes
    marinating)
No cooking required

1kg (2¼lb) tuna
Juice of 1 lime
1 garlic clove, crushed
5cm (2 inch) piece of ginger, grated
½ bunch of chives, finely chopped
1 tablespoon virtually fat-free fromage frais
Salt and black pepper

Cut the tuna up into small cubes and drizzle the lime
juice over them. Mix the garlic, ginger, chives and
fromage frais in a bowl. Season with salt and pepper
and add the fish. Mix thoroughly and leave in the
fridge for 15 minutes before serving.

TARTARE DE THON ET DE DORADE
(TUNA AND SEA BREAM TARTARE)

(6 servings)

Preparation time: 20 minutes (plus 15 minutes
  marinating)
No cooking required

400g (14oz) tuna
400g (14oz) sea bream fillets
1 tablespoon tarragon vinegar
Juice of 1 lime
Salt and black pepper
1 shallot, chopped
6 sprigs of dill, very finely chopped
6 teaspoons salmon roe
Pink peppercorns, ground
Dill, to garnish

Finely chop the tuna and the sea bream and drizzle
over the oil and lime juice. Season with salt and pepper.
Add the shallot and dill. Divide equally among the six
ramekin dishes. Refrigerate for 15 minutes, then turn
out. Put a spoonful of salmon roe over each portion,
sprinkle over some pink peppercorns and decorate
with the remaining dill. Serve on a bed of lettuce
(Cruise phase) or with slices of lime.

TERRINE DE THON (TUNA TERRINE)

(2 servings)

Preparation time: 15 minutes
Cooking time: 50 minutes

2 tins of tuna, in brine or spring water
2–3 tablespoons virtually fat-free fromage frais
2 eggs
Salt and black pepper
A few capers

Preheat the oven to 180°C/350°F/Gas 4.
Blend one and a half of the tins of tuna. Put the rest to one side. Add the fromage frais, eggs, pepper and salt, stirring them together thoroughly to produce a smooth mixture. Add the rest of the tuna and the capers. Pour this mixture into a cake tin lined with greaseproof and bake for 45–50 minutes.

LAMELLES CRUES DE BONITE (TUNA CARPACCIO)

(1–2 servings)

Preparation time: 15 minutes
No cooking required

300g (10½oz) raw tuna, slightly frozen
1 tablespoon soy sauce

1 tablespoon lemon juice
1 tablespoon tarragon vinegar
A few drops of Tabasco
1 tablespoon chopped herbs
Salt
Lemons, for garnish

Cut the slightly frozen fish into extremely thin strips. Prepare the dressing by mixing together the other ingredients and brush it over the fish. Serve on a plate decorated with lemons.

MÉLI-MÉLO DE THON
(SPICY TUNA)

(2 servings)

Preparation time: 10 minutes
No cooking required

475g (1lb 1oz) tuna, in brine or spring water
1 teaspoon capers, chopped
40g (1½oz) onion, chopped
1 tablespoon parsley
3 pinches of curry powder
A few drops of Tabasco

Drain the tuna and mix all the other ingredients together. With a fork, work the tuna into the mixture. Serve chilled.

PAIN DE POISSON (TUNA BREAD)

(2 servings)

Preparation time: 10 minutes
Cooking time: 40 minutes

300g (10½ oz) tuna, in brine or spring water
75g (2¾oz) cornflour
3 eggs
100ml (3½fl oz) skimmed milk
2 teaspoons yeast
Salt and black pepper

Preheat the oven to 200°C/400°F/Gas 6.
Chop up the tuna and mix it thoroughly with the other ingredients. Pour the mixture into a cake tin and bake for 40 minutes. Serve cold with a tomato sauce (in the Cruise phase) or *Dukan Mayonnaise* (see page 358).

THON GRILLÉ (GRILLED TUNA)

(2 servings)

Preparation time: 15 minutes
Cooking time: 10 minutes

2 sprigs of parsley, very finely chopped
1 small bunch of oregano, very finely chopped
1 small bunch of thyme, very finely chopped
3 or 4 bay leaves, crushed

Juice of 1 lemon
1 teaspoon mustard seeds
1 slice of tuna, weighing around 400–500g (14oz– 1lb 2oz)

In a bowl, stir the herbs, bay leaves, lemon juice and mustard seeds together thoroughly. Brush this marinade all over each side of the tuna slice. Grill the fish for 5 minutes on each side at a high temperature, moistening it all the while with the marinade.

AGAR-AGAR DE POISSON (FISH AGAR-AGAR)

(2 servings)

Preparation time: 15 minutes
Cooking time: 10 minutes

150ml (5fl oz) low-salt stock
Salt and black pepper
2g (1/16oz) agar-agar powder
3 white fish fillets, cut into pieces
Juice of ½ lemon

Over a gentle heat, warm 250ml (9fl oz) water with the stock, salt, pepper and agar-agar. After 5 minutes, put the fish fillets in the pan and continue cooking for a further 4 minutes with the pan covered. Before putting the mixture into a cake tin or two small moulds to set, stir it and then add the lemon juice. Leave to cool, then refrigerate. To turn the jelly out, submerge the mould carefully into some hot water, then ease out.

In the Cruise phase, you can serve with a warm tomato sauce.

GÂTEAU DE POISSON
(HERBY FISHCAKE)

(1 serving)

Preparation time: 10 minutes
Cooking time: 45 minutes

3 eggs, separated
6 tablespoons virtually fat-free quark
1 tablespoon cornflour
1 garlic clove, crushed
Herbs (parsley, chives)
1 nice fish fillet (cod, pollock or coley), chopped
3 seafood sticks (surimi), cut into thin slices
Salt and black pepper

Preheat the oven to 180°C/350°F/Gas 4.
Beat the egg whites until stiff and gently fold them into the yolks. Mix in the quark, cornflour, garlic, parsley and chives. Add the fish and the seafood sticks. Season. Put the mixture into a tin lined with greaseproof paper and bake for 45 minutes

Galettes

GALETTES SALÉES
(SAVOURY GALETTES)

(1 serving)

Preparation time: 20 minutes
Cooking time: 15 minutes

For the galette
2 tablespoons oat bran
1 tablespoon virtually fat-free fat fromage frais
50g (1¾oz) virtually fat-free quark
3 eggs, separated
Herbs, to taste
Salt and black pepper

For the filling (choose one)
175g (6oz) flaked tuna
200g (7oz) smoked salmon
150g (5½oz) extra-lean ham
150g (5½oz) extra-lean chopped meat

Mix together all the ingredients for the galette, except the egg whites, until the mixture is smooth. Add herbs to taste and season with salt and pepper. Finally, work in the filling chosen, along with the stiffly beaten egg whites. Once the mixture is ready, pour it into a warmed frying pan and cook over a medium heat, using a spatula to turn it over, and then continue cooking on the other side.

GALETTE SUCRÉES
(SWEET GALETTE)
(1 serving)

Preparation time: 20 minutes
Cooking time: 15 minutes

For the galette
2 tablespoons oat bran
1 tablespoon virtually fat-free fat fromage frais
50g (1¾oz) virtually fat-free quark
1 tablespoon sweetener
3 eggs, separated

For the filling (choose one)
2 tablespoons almond extract
2 tablespoons orange flower water
1 teaspoon fat-reduced cocoa, mixed with 1 egg yolk

Mix together all the ingredients for the galette, except the egg whites, until the mixture is smooth. Finally, work in the filling chosen, along with the stiffly beaten egg whites. Once the mixture is ready, pour it into a warmed frying pan and cook over a medium heat, using a spatula to turn it over, and then continue cooking on the other side. For the chocolate galette, cook the galette first then pour the chocolate mixture over it.

GALETTE À LA VIANDE DES GRISONS (BRESAOLA GALETTE)

(1 serving)

Preparation time: 20 minutes
Cooking time: 15 minutes

For the galette
2 tablespoons oat bran
1 tablespoon virtually fat-free fat fromage frais
50g (1¾oz) virtually fat-free quark
3 eggs, separated
Herbs, to taste
Salt and black pepper

For the topping
5 or 6 slices of bresaola
1 tablespoon virtually fat-free cottage cheese (optional)

Mix together all the ingredients for the galette, except the egg whites, until the mixture is smooth. Add herbs to taste and season with salt and pepper. Finally, work in the stiffly beaten egg whites. Once the mixture is ready, pour it into a warmed frying pan and cook over a medium heat, using a spatula to turn it over, and then continue cooking on the other side. Once the galette is cooked, spread the bresaola slices and tablespoon of cottage cheese on top.

LE PAIN DUKAN
(DUKAN BREAD)

(1 serving)

Preparation time: 5 minutes
Cooking time: 10 minutes

1 egg
15g (½oz) virtually fat-free fromage frais
15g (½oz) virtually fat-free quark
1 level tablespoon cornflour
1 teaspoon yeast
Dried herbs and spices, of your choice
Be careful not to add any salt!

Preheat the oven to 200°C/400°F/Gas 6 or use the microwave.
Mix together all the ingredients and pour them into

a rectangular tin measuring 15 x 20cm (6 x 8 inches). It must be at least 5mm (¼ inch) deep, if not, use a smaller tin. Bake in the oven for at least 10 minutes or, if using the microwave, cover with clingfilm and cook on maximum for 5 minutes. Once the bread is cooked, immediately remove the clingfilm and turn it out so that it does not sink back into the tin.

TARTE À LA CANNELLE (CINNAMON TART)
(4 servings)

Preparation time: 25 minutes
Cooking time: 40 minutes

For the base (using the galette recipe)
2 tablespoons oat bran
1 tablespoon virtually fat-free fat fromage frais
50g (1¾oz) virtually fat-free quark
I tablespoon sweetener
3 eggs, separated

For the topping
3 eggs
Aspartame, to taste
250g (9oz) virtually fat-free fromage frais and quark in
    equal quantities
1 tablespoon ground cinnamon
1 vanilla pod

Preheat the oven to 220°C/425°F/Gas 7.

Mix together all the ingredients for the base (this is the same as the galette recipe), except the egg whites, until the mixture is smooth. Finally, work in the stiffly beaten egg whites. Prepare the topping by breaking the eggs into a bowl and beating them. Add the aspartame (according to taste) and beat until the mixture has a creamy texture. Then work in the fromage frais, quark and cinnamon. Split open the vanilla pod and scrape out the seeds, adding them to the mixture. Line a cake tin with greaseproof paper. Pour the pastry mixture into the bottom of the tin and bake for 10 minutes. Pour the topping over the tart base and bake for a further 30 minutes.

Desserts

BAVAROIS DE FROMAGE BLANC À LA VANILLE (VANILLA FROMAGE FRAIS BAVAROIS)

(2 servings)

Preparation time: 15 minutes (plus overnight chilling)
No cooking required

3 gelatine leaves
2 egg whites
450g (1lb) virtually fat-free vanilla-flavoured fromage frais
Aspartame, to taste

Soak the gelatine leaves for 5 minutes in cold water. Beat the egg whites until stiff. Gently heat 3 tablespoons water. Wipe the gelatine leaves dry and place them in the hot water, stirring them so that they dissolve. Whip the fromage frais, add the stiffly beaten egg whites and the liquid gelatine and continue beating for 2–3 minutes. Sweeten with aspartame to taste. Refrigerate overnight.

GELÉE D'AMANDES
(ALMOND MILK JELLIES)

(2 servings)

Preparation time: 15 minutes (plus setting time)
Cooking time: 5 minutes

400ml (14fl oz) skimmed milk
6 drops of almond extract
3 gelatine leaves

Heat the milk and almond extract in a saucepan and bring to the boil. Soak the gelatine leaves in a bowl of cold water for a few minutes, drain them, then stir into the boiled milk, which has been taken off the heat. Stir until the gelatine has completely dissolved, pour it into one or two dishes, ensuring that the jelly is less than 1cm (½ inch) thick and leave to set in the fridge.

BLANC-MANGER (BLANCMANGE)

(4 servings)

Preparation time: 25 minutes (plus 2 hours
  refrigeration)
No cooking required

2 gelatine leaves
400g (14oz) virtually fat-free fromage frais
3 tablespoons sweetener
8–10 drops of almond extract
1 egg white

Soak the gelatine leaves for 5 minutes in a bowl of
cold water. In a small saucepan, warm 50g (1¾oz) of
the fromage frais over a gentle heat. Drain off the
gelatine, squeeze out any water and carefully stir it
into the fromage frais until it has completely dissolved.
Pour the rest of the fromage frais into a bowl along
with 2 tablespoons of the sweetener and the almond
extract, and beat until you have a smooth mixture,
then stir in the fromage frais and gelatine mixture.
Beat the egg white until stiff. When it is almost stiff,
add the rest of the sweetener and continue beating
for a few more seconds. Gently fold the egg white into
the fromage frais. Divide the mixture equally among
four ramekin dishes and refrigerate for at least 2 hours
before serving.

CHEESECAKE
(CHEESECAKE)
(2 servings)

Preparation time: 10 minutes
Cooking time: 12 minutes

5 tablespoons virtually fat-free fromage frais
2 tablespoons cornflour
2 egg yolks
2 tablespoons lemon juice
3 tablespoons sweetener
5 egg whites

Beat together the fromage frais, cornflour, egg yolks, lemon and sweetener until the mixture is frothy. Beat the egg whites until stiff, then carefully fold them into the fromage frais mixture and pour this into a soufflé dish. Cook for 12 minutes in the microwave on medium power. Eat cold.

COOKIES (COOKIES)

(1 serving)

Preparation time: 10 minutes
Cooking time: 20 minutes

2 eggs, separated
½ teaspoon liquid sweetener
20 drops of vanilla extract
2 tablespoons oat bran

Preheat the oven to 180°C/350°F/Gas 4.
In a bowl, mix together the 2 egg yolks, sweetener, vanilla and oat bran. Beat the egg whites until very stiff and carefully fold them into the bran mixture, then pour this into a flat baking tin. Place in the oven and bake for 15–20 minutes.

BISCUIT DE SAVOIE (SAVOY BISCUIT)

(2 servings)

Preparation time: 30 minutes
Cooking time: 40 minutes

3 eggs, separated
6 tablespoons aspartame
1 tablespoon vanilla extract
7 tablespoons cornflour
1 teaspoon yeast

Preheat the oven to 180°C/350°F/Gas 4.

In a bowl, beat together the egg yolks with the aspartame and vanilla extract until the mixture is creamy. Add the cornflour and yeast. Beat the egg whites until stiff and fold them in. Pour into a sandwich tin measuring 22–24cm (9–9½ inches) lined with greaseproof paper. Bake for 35–40 minutes. Turn out whilst still warm and leave to cool on a rack.

CRÈME AU COFFEE
(COFFEE CREAM)

(4 servings)

Preparation time: 5 minutes
Cooking time: 25 minutes

600ml (1 pint) skimmed milk
1 teaspoon instant coffee
3 eggs
3 tablespoons sweetener

Preheat the oven to 140°C/275F/Gas 1.

Boil the milk and coffee together. Beat the eggs and sweetener and gradually add the milk and coffee mixture, stirring continuously. Pour the mixture into four ramekin dishes, place into a bigger dish and fill this *bain-marie* half full with cold water. Bake for 20 minutes. Serve cold.

CRÈME AUX SPICES
(SPICY CREAM)

(4 servings)

Preparation time: 20 minutes (plus chilling time)
Cooking time: 20 minutes

250ml (9fl oz) skimmed milk
1 vanilla pod
½ teaspoon ground cinnamon
1 clove
1 star anise
2 egg yolks
2 tablespoons sweetener
200g (7oz) virtually fat-free fromage frais

Put the milk, vanilla pod split in two lengthways, cinnamon, clove and star anise into a saucepan and bring to the boil. In a bowl, beat the egg yolks with the sweetener until the mixture turns pale. Pour the hot milk little by little over the egg yolks, stirring continuously. Pour the mixture back into the saucepan and cook for 12 minutes over a gentle heat, stirring frequently until the cream coats the spoon. Strain the cream and allow to cool. Work the fromage frais into the cooled cream. Refrigerate and serve cold.

CRÈME À LA VANILLE (VANILLA CREAM)

(2 servings)

Preparation time: 15 minutes
Cooking time: 20 minutes

500ml (18fl oz) skimmed milk
3 eggs
50g (1¾oz) aspartame
A few drops of vanilla essence
A pinch of grated nutmeg

Preheat the oven to 180°C/350°F/Gas 4.
Line a baking dish with a sheet of greaseproof paper.
Whisk together the milk, eggs, sweetener and vanilla.
Pour this mixture into the dish and sprinkle with
nutmeg. Place the dish into a bigger dish and fill this
bain-marie half full with cold water. Bake in the oven
for 20 minutes until the cream is firm to the touch.
Serve warm or cold.

CRÈME FOUETTÉE (CREAMY WHIP)

(1 serving)

Preparation time: 5 minutes
No cooking required

60g (2¼oz) virtually fat-free fromage frais
60g (2¼oz) virtually fat-free quark

1 tablespoon aspartame
2 egg whites

Beat together the fromage frais, quark and sweetener. Gently fold in the very stiffly beaten egg whites. Serve cold.

CRÈME JAPONAISE (JAPANESE CREAM)
(1 serving)

Preparation time: 5 minutes (plus chilling time)
No cooking required

10g (¼oz) powdered skimmed milk
1 pinch of instant coffee
¼ teaspoon powdered gelatine
Sweetener, to taste

Reconstitute the milk with 100ml (3½fl oz) water. Flavour with the coffee and heat without allowing it to boil. Allow the gelatine to soften and swell in 3 tablespoons cold water and add to the milk with the sweetener. Place in a sundae dish and refrigerate until set.

DESSERT LISALINE
(LISALINE DESSERT)

(2 servings)

Preparation time: 20 minutes
Cooking time: 40 minutes

2 eggs, separated
6 tablespoons virtually fat-free fromage frais
Liquid sweetener, to taste
1 teaspoon lemon juice (or orange flower water)

Preheat the oven to 180°C/350°F/Gas 4.
Whisk together the egg yolks, fromage frais, sweetener and lemon juice until it is nice and smooth. Beat the egg whites until stiff. Gently fold the egg yolk mixture into the stiffly beaten egg whites. Pour the mixture into ramekin dishes and bake for 25–30 minutes, then brown under the grill for 5–10 minutes, keeping a careful eye that the dessert does not burn.

DESSERT MOUZETTE
(MOUZETTE DESSERT)

(4 servings)

Preparation time: 15 minutes (plus 1 hour chilling
    time)
No cooking required

3 gelatine leaves
2 tablespoons lemon juice
300g (10½oz) virtually fat-free fromage frais
2 eggs, separated
Sweetener, to taste

Soak the gelatine leaves in a bowl of cold water for a few minutes. Warm the lemon juice over a gentle heat. Drain the gelatine and dissolve in the lemon juice, then leave to cool. Mix together the fromage frais with the 2 egg yolks and sweetener, then add the lemon juice. Beat the egg whites until stiff, then gently fold them into the rest of the mixture. Place in a small bowl, in the fridge, for 1 hour to set.

FLAN
(NUTMEG CUSTARDS)

(4–5 servings)

Preparation time: 15 minutes
Cooking time: 50 minutes

5 eggs
375ml (13fl oz) skimmed milk
1 vanilla pod
1 pinch of ground nutmeg

Preheat the oven to 190°C/375°F/Gas 5.

Beat the eggs in a large bowl. Heat the milk with the vanilla pod without letting it come to the boil. Pour the hot milk gently over the eggs and add the ground nutmeg. Pour the mixture into ramekin dishes and bake for 45 minutes, keeping a careful eye on the custards.

GÂTEAU AU FROMAGE BLANC (FROMAGE FRAIS GATEAU)

(4 servings)

Preparation time: 10 minutes
Cooking time: 30 minutes

125g (4½oz) virtually fat-free fromage frais
25g (1oz) cornflour
1 teaspoon yeast
Grated zest of 1 lemon
½ teaspoon sweetener
2 egg yolks
4 egg whites
3 drops of oil

Preheat the oven to 200°C/400°F/Gas 6.

Mix together all the ingredients except for the egg whites and oil. Little by little, fold the four stiffly beaten egg whites into the mixture. Pour into a cake tin (oiled and wiped with kitchen paper) and cook for 30 minutes. To be eaten cold.

GÂTEAU AU YAOURT
(ORANGE YOGHURT CAKE)

(2 servings)

Preparation time: 15 minutes
Cooking time: 45 minutes

3 eggs
150g (5½oz) fat-free natural yoghurt
½ teaspoon sweetener
1 teaspoon orange extract
4 tablespoons cornflour
2 teaspoons yeast
3 drops of oil

Preheat the oven to 180°C/350°F/Gas 4.
Beat the eggs together with the yoghurt, then add the sweetener, orange extract, cornflour and yeast. Pour into a cake tin (oiled and wiped with kitchen paper) and bake for 45 minutes.

MOELLEUX AU YAOURT
(BAKED YOGHURT PUDDING)

(4 servings)

Preparation time: 15 minutes

Cooking time: 30 minutes

2 eggs, separated

2 teaspoons sweetener

300g (10½oz) fat-free natural yoghurt

50g (1¾oz) cornflour

Flavouring of your choice (lemon zest, cinnamon,
    coffee)

1 pinch of salt

Preheat the oven to 220°C/425°F/Gas 7.

Mix together the egg yolks and sweetener. Add the
yoghurt, cornflour and flavouring. Beat the egg whites
with a pinch of salt until very stiff. Gently fold them
into the mixture. Pour the mixture into an 18cm (7
inch) cake tin and bake for 20–30 minutes.

GÂTEAU NANA
(NANA'S CAKE)

(2 servings)

Preparation time: 15 minutes
Cooking time: 35 minutes

2 heaped tablespoons cornflour
½ teaspoon sweetener
Grated zest of 1 lemon
3 eggs, separated
3 heaped tablespoons virtually fat-free fromage frais
3 drops of oil

Preheat the oven to 180°C/350°F/Gas 4.
Blend the cornflour, sweetener and lemon zest into the egg yolks. Mix together thoroughly. Add the stiffly beaten egg whites to the mixture. Pour into a cake tin or some ramekin dishes (oiled and wiped with kitchen paper) and bake for 30–35 minutes.

GÉNOISE (SPONGE CAKE)

(2 servings)

Preparation time: 10 minutes
Cooking time: 20 minutes

4 eggs, separated
100g (3½oz) aspartame
Zest of 1 lemon
40g (1½oz) cornflour

Preheat the oven to 180°C/350°F/Gas 4.
Beat the egg whites until stiff. Mix together the egg yolks and aspartame, add the zest and cornflour. Carefully fold in the stiffly beaten egg whites. Pour into a tin lined with greaseproof paper and bake for 20 minutes until the cake is golden brown.

GRANITÉ DE CAFÉ À LA CANNELLE (COFFEE AND CINNAMON GRANITA)

(2 servings)

Preparation time: 10 minutes
No cooking required

500ml (18fl oz) hot black coffee
Sweetener, to taste
1 teaspoon ground cinnamon
3 cardamom seeds

Mix together the hot coffee, sweetener and spices. Stir and leave to cool. Pour into a dish and freeze for about 1 hour. Blend the mixture for 1 minute, then return it to the dish. Refrigerate for about 15 minutes. Divide the granita between two sundae dishes and serve.

SORBET AU THÉ (TEA SORBET)

(2 servings)

Preparation time: 20 minutes (plus freezing time)
No cooking required

You will need an ice cream machine.

3 tablespoons China tea
Juice of 1 lemon
4 fresh mint leaves

Boil 300ml (10fl oz) water, add the tea to it, cover and leave to infuse for 3 minutes. Strain 4 tablespoons of the infusion and pour it into a flat dish that can be put in the freezer. Freeze, stirring with a fork occasionally until ice crystals start to form. Strain the remaining tea infusion through a strainer and pour into an ice cream machine along with the lemon juice. Churn for about 15 minutes. When ready to serve, fill some glasses (champagne flutes for example) with the sorbet, creating a dome shape. Scatter the iced tea crystals on top and finish off with a mint leaf.

SORBET AU CITRON VERT (LIME SORBET)
(2–3 servings)

Preparation time: 10 minutes (plus chilling time)
No cooking required

You will need an ice cream machine.

4 limes
500g (1lb 2oz) virtually fat-free fromage frais
3 tablespoons aspartame

Whiz up the zest from one of the limes in a blender. Add the fromage frais, juice from the other limes and the aspartame and blend. Refrigerate for 4 hours. Churn in an ice cream machine until ready.

SORBET AU YAOURT
(YOGHURT SORBET)
(2 or 3 servings)

Preparation time: 2 minutes (plus chilling time)
No cooking required

You will need an ice cream machine.

750g (1lb 10oz) fat-free natural yoghurt
Grated zest and juice of 2 lemons
2 tablespoons virtually fat-free fromage frais

Whisk the yoghurt. Add the grated lemon zest, then the lemon juice and fromage frais. Mix together well, pour into an ice cream machine and churn until the sorbet is ready.

LASSI SALÉ
(SALTED LASSI)

(4 servings)

Preparation time: 5 minutes
No cooking required

600g (1¼lb) fat-free natural yoghurt
500ml (18fl oz) skimmed milk
1 pinch of salt
¼ teaspoon crushed green cardamom
3 drops of rose water

Mix together all the ingredients and beat with a whisk. Pour the lassi into attractive glasses and keep in the fridge until ready to drink.

MOUSSE AU CAFÉ
(COFFEE MOUSSE)

(6 servings)

Preparation time: 10 minutes (plus 3 hours chilling)
No cooking required

90g (3oz) virtually fat-free fromage frais
90g (3oz) virtually fat-free quark
2 tablespoons sweetener
4 egg whites
1 tablespoon coffee essence

Whisk together the fromage frais and quark until the mixture is light. Add the sweetener. Beat the egg whites until stiff, carefully fold them into the mixture and finally add the coffee essence. Pour into ramekin dishes and leave to cool in the fridge for 3 hours.

MOUSSE AU CITRON
LEMON MOUSSE

(4 servings)

Preparation time: 20 minutes (plus chilling time)
Cooking time: 2 minutes

2 gelatine leaves
2 tablespoons sweetener
Grated zest of ½ lemon

250g (9oz) virtually fat-free fromage frais
1 egg, separated

Soak the gelatine leaves in a bowl of cold water for a few minutes. Add the sweetener, lemon zest and 50g (1¾oz) of the fromage frais to the egg yolk. Whisk together until the mixture is smooth and straw-coloured. Pour the mixture into a small saucepan and warm over a gentle heat for 2 minutes, then remove from the heat and stir in the carefully drained and squeezed gelatine. Mix together until completely dissolved. Whisk the remaining fromage frais until smooth and fold it into the lemon cream. Beat the egg white until stiff. Gently fold the beaten egg white into the lemon cream. Refrigerate for a couple of hours until set.

MOUSSE DE YAOURT À LA CANNELLE (CINNAMON YOGHURT MOUSSE)

(4 servings)

Preparation time: 15 minutes (plus chilling time)
No cooking required

4 eggs, separated
600g (1¼lb) fat-free natural yoghurt
1 teaspoon ground cinnamon
3 tablespoons sweetener

Beat the egg whites until stiff. In a bowl, beat the yoghurt, then add the cinnamon and sweetener. Gently fold in the stiffly beaten egg whites and put the mousse in the fridge to set for a couple of hours.

MOUSSE GLACÉE AU CITRON (ICED LEMON MOUSSE)

(2–3 servings)

Preparation time: 10 minutes (plus freezing time)
No cooking required

4 egg whites
500g (1lb 2oz) virtually fat-free fromage frais
Zest of 1 lemon
Juice of 5 lemons

Beat the egg whites until stiff. Whisk the fromage frais and carefully mix together with the lemon zest, lemon juice and egg whites. Place the mousse in a dish and freeze until it has set firm.

OEUFS À LA NEIGE
(FLOATING MERINGUES)

(2 servings)

Preparation time: 20 minutes
Cooking time: 10 minutes

250ml (9fl oz) skimmed milk
2 eggs, separated
1 tablespoon sweetener

Bring the milk to the boil. Beat the egg yolks and add the sweetener to them. Gradually stir in the boiling milk. Pour the mixture back into the saucepan and warm over a gentle heat, stirring all the time with a wooden spoon and making sure that nothing sticks to the bottom of the pan. As soon as the cream starts to set, remove the saucepan from the heat. The cream will curdle if allowed to come to the boil. Next, beat the egg whites until stiff. Using a tablespoon, place balls of egg white into a saucepan of boiling water. As soon as the egg whites start to swell up, remove them with a draining spoon and leave them to drain on some muslin. Once the custard has completely cooled down, arrange the egg whites on top and serve.

OEUFS AU LAIT
(MILKY EGGS)

(2 servings)

Preparation time: 10 minutes
Cooking time: 40 minutes

1 vanilla pod
500ml (18fl oz) skimmed milk
60g (2¼oz) sweetener
4 eggs

Preheat the oven to 220°C/425°F/Gas 7.
Split the vanilla pod in two, add to the milk along with
the sweetener and bring to the boil. Whisk the eggs
together in a bowl. Remove the vanilla from the milk
and very slowly pour the hot milk over the beaten
eggs, stirring all the time. Transfer this mixture to a
baking dish. Place the dish into a bigger dish and fill
this *bain-marie* half full with cold water. Cook for 40
minutes. Serve cold.

MUFFINS (MUFFINS)

(4 servings)

Preparation time: 10 minutes
Cooking time: 30 minutes

4 eggs, separated
8 tablespoons oat bran
4 tablespoons virtually fat-free fromage frais
½ teaspoon sweetener
Flavouring of your choice (lemon zest, cinnamon,
    coffee)

Preheat the oven to 180°C/350°F/Gas 4.
Beat the egg whites until stiff. Mix together all the
other ingredients, then gently fold in the stiffly beaten
egg whites. Pour into a muffin tin and bake for 20–30
minutes.

TARTE AU CITRON (LEMON TART)

(6 servings)

Preparation time: 15 minutes
Cooking time: 35 minutes

3 eggs, separated
Sweetener, to taste
Grated zest and juice of 1 lemon
1 pinch of salt

Preheat the oven to 180°C/350°F/Gas 4.

Beat the egg yolks with a pinch of sweetener. Add 2 tablespoons water, the lemon juice and zest. Place the dish into a bigger dish and fill this bain-marie half full with cold water. Cook over a gentle heat, stirring together with a spatula until the mixture thickens. Remove from the heat. Add the salt and sweetener (according to taste) to the egg whites and beat until stiff. Carefully fold the egg whites into the hot egg yolks. Pour the mixture into a non-stick baking dish, measuring 28cm (11 inches) in diameter. Bake until golden brown on top.

RECIPES WITH
PROTEINS AND VEGETABLES

Soups

SOUPE DE CONCOMBRE GLACÉE
AUX CREVETTES ROSES
(ICED CUCUMBER SOUP WITH PRAWNS)

(4 servings)

Preparation time: 30 minutes
No cooking required

2 small cucumbers, deseeded
1 onion
1 garlic clove
Juice of 2 lemons
2 tablespoons anisette (aniseed-flavoured liquor)
    (optional)
Salt and black pepper
4 sprigs of coriander, very finely chopped
8 large prawns, cooked and shelled
A few drops of Tabasco
¼ red pepper, deseeded and very thinly sliced
½ red onion, deseeded and very thinly sliced

Whiz the cucumber finely in a blender with the onion, garlic clove, juice of 1 lemon, anisette, salt and pepper. Dilute this purée with 400–500ml (14–18fl oz) spring water. Add half the coriander and put in the fridge for 45 minutes. Thirty minutes before you are ready to serve, split the prawns lengthways and spread them out on a plate. Sprinkle over the juice of 1 lemon and a few drops of Tabasco, cover and put them back in the fridge for 30 minutes. Adjust the seasoning for the soup and divide it among four large bowls. Arrange the pepper and onion slices, prawns and remaining coriander on top. Serve immediately.

SOUPE DE CREVETTES AU CONCOMBRE ET À LA CORIANDRE
(PRAWN SOUP WITH CUCUMBER AND CORIANDER)

(4 servings)

Preparation time: 15 minutes
Cooking time: 12 minutes

2 low-salt chicken stock cubes
1 cucumber, peeled and thinly sliced
2 onions, thinly sliced
12 nice large Mediterranean prawns, shelled but tails on
3 sprigs of parsley, very finely chopped
2 sprigs of coriander, very finely chopped
1 small chilli, very finely chopped

Bring 1.5 litres (2½ pints) water to the boil in a casserole dish and dissolve the stock cubes. Add the cucumber, onion and prawns. When the stock comes to the boil again, cook for 2 minutes. Sprinkle the herbs and tiny bits of chilli on top and serve hot.

SOUPE DE CONCOMBRE
(CHILLED CUCUMBER SOUP)

(1 serving)

Preparation time: 10 minutes
No cooking required

½ cucumber
1 garlic clove
Salt and black pepper
1 tablespoon tomato purée
A few drops of Tabasco
1 tablespoon virtually fat-free fromage frais
Ice cubes

Peel the cucumber and whiz in a blender with the garlic and some salt and pepper. Add the tomato purée, Tabasco, according to taste, fromage frais and ice cubes. Serve chilled.

SOUPE À LA CAROTTE, FENOUIL ET THYM (CARROT, FENNEL AND THYME SOUP)

(3 servings)

Preparation time: 20 minutes
Cooking time: 25 minutes

350g (12oz) onions, diced
350g (12oz) leeks, diced
2 garlic cloves, very finely chopped
¼ teaspoon fennel seeds
½ teaspoon thyme
4 medium carrots, diced
1 fennel bulb, diced (plus fennel tops to garnish)
1 litre (1¾ pints) low-salt chicken stock
Salt and black pepper

Over a medium heat, in a high-sided frying pan (oiled and wiped with kitchen paper), gently fry the onion, leek, garlic, fennel seeds and thyme until the mixture smells aromatic. Add the carrot and fennel and cook for a few more minutes. Add the stock and season with salt and pepper. Cook until the carrot and fennel are soft. If the stock goes down too much, add some water. When ready to serve, place a little chopped fennel top in each bowl of soup.

SOUPE VERTE À L'OSEILLE
(GREEN SORREL SOUP)

(4 servings)

Preparation time: 35 minutes
Cooking time: 30 minutes

2 eggs
1 onion, chopped
2 leeks (white part only), thinly sliced
5–6 lettuce leaves, chopped
1 bunch of sorrel, chopped
250g (9oz) spinach, chopped
Salt and black pepper
2 low-salt chicken stock cubes
3 chives, finely chopped
1 sprig of chervil, finely chopped

Cook the eggs for 10 minutes in boiling water until hard-boiled. Fry the onion and leek in a high-sided frying pan (oiled and wiped with kitchen paper) over a medium heat. Add the other vegetables and allow them to soften over a gentle heat for 5 minutes whilst stirring. Pour in 1 litre (1¾pints) hot water, season with salt and pepper and add the stock cubes. Continue cooking for 10 minutes over a medium heat. Shell the hard-boiled eggs and chop them up finely. Whiz the soup in a blender and sprinkle the chopped eggs and herbs over the soup before serving.

VELOUTÉ DE COURGETTES
(CREAM OF COURGETTE SOUP)

(1 serving)

Preparation time: 10 minutes
Cooking time: 30 minutes

1 low-salt chicken stock cube
3–4 courgettes
25g (1oz) virtually fat-free quark
Salt and black pepper

Put 350ml (12fl oz) water in a saucepan with the stock cube, dissolve the cube, then add the unpeeled, grated courgettes. Cover and cook over a medium heat for 30 minutes, stirring all the time. Remove from the heat, add the quark, adjust the seasoning and stir well before blending the mixture in a blender.

VELOUTÉ GLACÉ AUX COURGETTES
(ICED CREAMED COURGETTE SOUP)

(1 serving)

Preparation time: 7 minutes
Cooking time: 10 minutes

2 medium courgettes
2 low-salt chicken stock cubes
300g (10½oz) fat-free natural yoghurt

Salt and black pepper
Ice cubes
6 basil leaves, chopped

Cut the courgettes into slices, but do not remove the skin. Place in a small casserole dish of salted, boiling water and simmer for 8 minutes. In the meantime, bring to the boil 200ml (7fl oz) water with the stock cubes. Remove from the heat and leave on one side. Drain and rinse the courgettes, then whiz them with the stock in a blender. Add 400ml (14fl oz) iced water, then the yoghurt. Mix together and adjust the seasoning. Refrigerate until ready to serve. Serve the soup very cold by adding a few ice cubes to it and sprinkle the basil on top.

SOUPE AU CITRON À LA GRECQUE
(GREEK LEMON SOUP)

(2 servings)

Preparation time: 10 minutes
Cooking time: 10 minutes

2 low-salt chicken stock cubes
1 pinch of saffron
2 carrots
2 courgettes
1–2 egg yolks
Zest and juice of 1 lemon

Bring 1 litre (1¾ pints) water to the boil with the chicken stock cubes and saffron. In the meantime, roughly grate the carrots and courgettes separately. Put the carrot in the stock and boil for 5 minutes. Add the courgette and boil for 3 minutes. Add 1 or 2 egg yolks, the lemon juice and grated lemon zest. Continue cooking over a medium heat, but do not allow the soup to boil.

SOUPE AU CONCOMBRE (QUICK GAZPACHO)
(1 serving)

Preparation time: 15 minutes
No cooking required

4 tomatoes
1 red pepper
1 green pepper
2 cucumbers, peeled, deseeded and cut
Some mint
Salt and black pepper

Poach the tomatoes in boiling water for 30 seconds, then peel and deseed them. Grill the peppers for 10–15 minutes until charred all over. Place in a plastic bag and leave to cool, before peeling away the skin and seeds and cutting into chunks. Blend the tomato, pepper and cucumber together with the mint in a blender. Season according to taste and serve chilled.

SOUPE GLACÉE À LA TOMATE
(ICED TOMATO SOUP)

(4 servings)

Preparation time: 20 minutes
No cooking required

1kg (2¼lb) tomatoes, deseeded and cut into quarters
3 parsley stalks
1 sprig of basil
1 onion, quartered
1 garlic clove chopped
1 sprig of thyme
1 sprig of savory or oregano
Salt and black pepper

Reduce the tomatoes to a fine purée, with the parsley, basil, onion and garlic. Remove the thyme and savory leaves and stir them into the tomato purée. Add salt and pepper. Pour the soup into a soup tureen and put it in the fridge to cool. Serve chilled.

POTAGE ACIDULÉ (TANGY TOMATO SOUP)

(2 servings)

Preparation time: 15 minutes (plus 1 hour chilling)
No cooking required

1 lemon
600g (1¼lb) tomatoes, roughly chopped
200g (7oz) carrots, roughly chopped
1 stick of celery, with the leaves, roughly chopped
A few drops of Tabasco
Salt and black pepper

Wash the lemon, peel half of it, then cut it up into small cubes. Place the tomato, carrot, celery and lemon in a blender and whiz together. Season with salt and pepper and add the Tabasco. Leave to chill for 1 hour in the fridge.

POTAGE AU FENOUIL (FENNEL SOUP)

(3 servings)

Preparation time: 20 minutes
Cooking time: 50 minutes

3 fennel bulbs, thinly sliced
1 litre (1¾ pints) low-salt chicken stock
4 ripe tomatoes
3 shallots, peeled

2 garlic cloves, peeled
A few sprigs of thyme
1 small bay leaf
Salt and black pepper
50g (1¾oz) virtually fat-free fromage frais
A few sprigs of parsley, chopped

Cook the fennel, covered, over a medium heat in the stock and 500ml (18fl oz) water for about 20 minutes. Whilst the fennel is cooking, poach the tomatoes in boiling water for 30 seconds, then peel and deseed them. Blend the tomatoes in a food processor with the shallots and garlic cloves, then add this mixture to the fennel soup along with the thyme, bay leaf and seasoning. Continue cooking for 30 minutes. When ready to serve, stir in the fromage frais and parsley.

POTAGE AUX ENDIVES
(CHICORY AND SMOKED CHICKEN SOUP)

(4 servings)

Preparation time: 15 minutes
Cooking time: 25 minutes

800g (1¾lb) chicory, chopped
1 litre (1¾ pints) low-salt chicken stock
1 onion, chopped
100g (3½ oz) smoked chicken slices, cut into small
    pieces

Cook the chicory in the stock for 10 minutes over a medium heat. Using a different pan, gently fry the onion and small smoked chicken pieces. As soon as the chicory is cooked, add the onion and chicken to the stock and cook for a few minutes more over a medium heat before serving.

SOUPE DE POULET AUX CHAMPIGNONS (CHICKEN AND MUSHROOM SOUP)

(4 servings)

Preparation time: 20 minutes
Cooking time: 15 minutes

1 garlic clove
1 tablespoon coriander leaves
1 teaspoon pepper
100g (3½oz) button mushrooms, thinly sliced
3 drops of oil
1 litre (1¾ pints) low-salt chicken stock
2 tablespoons nuoc mam (Vietnamese fish sauce)
250g (9oz) cooked chicken breast, cut into thin slices
2 shallots, finely chopped

Crush the garlic, coriander and pepper into a purée in a pestle and mortar. Place the mushroom in a non-stick frying pan (oiled and wiped with kitchen paper) and fry the mixture for 1 minute over a medium heat.

Remove from the heat and keep to one side. Bring the stock to the boil in a saucepan, add the mushroom, nuoc mam and garlic purée. Cover and gently simmer for 5 minutes. Add the chicken to the mixture, cook for a few minutes, then garnish with the shallot.

POTAGE D'AUBERGINE AU CURRY ROUGE (RED CURRIED AUBERGINE SOUP)

(2 servings)

Preparation time: 20 minutes
Cooking time: 45 minutes

1 aubergine
3 drops of oil
1 red onion, chopped
1 chilli, very finely chopped
1 tablespoon curry powder
½ teaspoon ground cinnamon
¼ clove, ground
Salt and black pepper
250g (9oz) chopped tomatoes
750ml (1¼ pints) low-salt vegetable stock

Chop off the ends of the aubergine and cut it into 2.5cm (1 inch) thick slices. In a large saucepan (oiled and wiped with kitchen paper), gently brown the onion over a medium heat for 3 minutes, then add the chilli, curry powder, cinnamon and clove. Add some salt and gently fry for another 2 minutes, then add the aubergine, tomatoes and stock. Simmer for 40 minutes with the saucepan half covered, put to one side and leave to cool. Whiz the soup in a blender and heat it through again gently. Adjust the seasoning to taste.

POTAGE DE NAVETS AU CURRY (CURRIED TURNIP SOUP WITH CRISPY HAM)

(2 servings)

Preparation time: 20 minutes
Cooking time: 50 minutes

1kg (2¼lb) turnips
1 onion, roughly chopped
4 garlic cloves, thinly sliced
3 drops of oil
1 pinch of curry powder
900ml (1½ pints) low-salt chicken stock
Salt and black pepper
A few drops of Tabasco
Juice of ½ lemon
200g (7oz) fat-fat natural yoghurt
70g (2½oz) extra-lean thin ham slices
2 sprigs of parsley (or chives), finely chopped
1 pinch of nutmeg

Peel and remove the hard centre core of the turnips. Sweat the onion and garlic in a cast-iron casserole dish (oiled and wiped with kitchen paper) over a medium heat. Cover and cook for 5 minutes, then add the turnip. Mix together well, cover and cook for 10 minutes, keeping a careful eye on the dish. Stir in the curry powder, mix it into the vegetables and pour in the stock. Leave to simmer away gently for about 30 minutes, then whiz in a blender (bearing in mind that this soup is meant to have a fine texture). Adjust the seasoning and add a few drops of Tabasco and the lemon juice. Heat the soup though again and stir in 150g (5½oz) of the yoghurt. In the meantime, fry the ham in its own juices in a frying pan, drain on some kitchen paper and crumble it between your fingers. Serve the soup with a little extra yoghurt, sprinkling over the crispy ham, parsley and nutmeg.

BOUILLON DE LÉGUMES D'EUGÉNIE
(EUGÉNIE'S VEGETABLE BOUILLON)

(1 serving)

Preparation time: 15 minutes
Cooking time: 10 minutes

2 medium tomatoes
1.2 litres (2 pints) low-salt strong-flavoured chicken
 stock
Salt and black pepper
50g (1¾oz) carrots, cut into long, thin julienne strips
50g (1¾oz) button mushrooms, cut into long, thin
 julienne strips
25g (1oz) sticks of celery, cut into long, thin julienne
 strips
25g (1oz) leek (white part only), cut into long, thin
 julienne strips
1 bunch of parsley, very finely chopped

Cut the tomatoes into quarters, deseed them, getting
rid of any liquid, then chop them up roughly into
chunks. Bring the stock to the boil and season with salt
and pepper. Add the vegetables (except the tomatoes)
to the stock and cook for 5–6 minutes without a lid on
(the vegetables should retain their bite). Remove the
pan from the heat, add the tomato and parsley and
serve hot.

Poultry and vegetables

BOUCHÉES AU POULET FUMÉ
(SMOKED CHICKEN MOUTHFULS)

(2 servings)

Preparation time: 45 minutes
Cooking time: 20 minutes

7 egg whites
1 tablespoon cornflour
175g (6oz) smoked chicken breast, diced
200g (7oz) button mushrooms, chopped
2 shallots, chopped
3 drops of oil
2 tablespoons virtually fat-free fromage frais
1 tablespoon chives, chopped
Salt and black pepper
20 chives, boiled to make them more supple

Whisk together the egg whites, 4 tablespoons cold water and the cornflour. Warm a non-stick frying pan and cook this mixture, spoonful by spoonful, to produce twenty round galettes, about 10cm (4 inches) in diameter. Drain on kitchen paper and keep warm. Over a medium heat, brown the chicken, mushroom and shallot in a frying pan (oiled and wiped with kitchen paper). Lower the heat, add the fromage frais, sprinkle in the chopped chives and season. Divide this topping among the galettes, fold them over like turnovers and tie each one together with a chive. Keep in a cool place and serve at room temperature.

BROCHETTES TIKKA
(TIKKA KEBABS)
(4 servings)

Preparation time: 25 minutes (plus 2 hours marinating)
Cooking time: 10 minutes

You will need kebab sticks (soak in a little water if using wooden sticks so that they do not burn when the meat is being cooked).

1 onion
1 garlic clove
20g (¾oz) piece of ginger, grated
2 tablespoons lemon juice
Salt and black pepper
100g (3½oz) fat-free natural yoghurt
½ tablespoon ground coriander

½ tablespoon ground cumin
1 teaspoon garam masala
2 tablespoons coriander, very finely chopped
800g (1¾lb) chicken breasts, cut into 2cm (¾ inch)
   chunks
Onion
Lemon wedges
Cucumber wedges

Peel the onion and garlic and reduce to a purée in a blender. Add the ginger, lemon juice, salt, yoghurt, all the spices and the coriander, then mix together well. Leave the chicken chunks to marinate in this sauce for 2 hours in the fridge. Thread the chicken chunks onto the kebab sticks and grill them for 8–10 minutes, turning them over regularly. Serve hot, accompanied by onion, lemon and cucumber.

FRICASSÉE DE POULET AUX CHAMPIGNONS ET AUX ASPERGES
(CHICKEN WITH MUSHROOMS AND ASPARAGUS)

(4 servings)

Preparation time: 20 minutes
Cooking time: 20 minutes

1kg (2¼lb) button mushrooms
2 mild onions, very thinly sliced

1kg (2¼lb) chicken breasts, cut into cubes
500g (1lb 2oz) asparagus tips, cut into small pieces
1 lemon
Salt and black pepper
Parsley (or chervil), chopped

In a non-stick frying pan, fry the mushrooms over a gentle heat and put to one side. Brown the onion over a gentle heat. Add the chicken and brown the meat for 6 minutes. Add the asparagus, then the mushrooms, lemon juice, salt, pepper and parsley. Cover and continue cooking over a medium heat for 10–12 minutes.

FRICASSÉE DE VOLAILLE À LA MARTINIQUAISE (MARTINIQUE CHICKEN FRICASSEE)

(4 servings)

Preparation time: 20 minutes
Cooking time: 55 minutes

1kg (2¼lb) chicken, halved
Salt and black pepper
3 drops of oil
250g (9oz) button mushrooms
4 tomatoes, cut into quarters
2 egg yolks
250g (9oz) virtually fat-free fromage frais

Season the chicken with salt and pepper and brown in a casserole dish (oiled and wiped with kitchen paper) over a medium heat for 10 minutes. Add the mushrooms, cover and cook for 40 minutes. After 30 minutes, add the tomato quarters. Put the egg yolks in a small glass bowl, add the fromage frais and mix together well. Take two ladlefuls of the cooking sauce and add to the bowl, mixing everything together thoroughly. Heat this sauce in a *bain-marie* or by placing the bowl over a pan of simmering water, then pour it over the skinned chicken.

PAPILLOTES DE POULET AUX COURGETTES (OVEN-BAKED CHICKEN PARCELS WITH COURGETTES)

(4 servings)

Preparation time: 10 minutes
Cooking time: 25 minutes

2 tomatoes
4 courgettes, cut into strips
1 garlic clove, chopped
1 lemon, thinly sliced
8 chicken breasts, cut into tiny strips

Preheat the oven to 220°C/425°C/Gas 7.
Poach the tomatoes in boiling water for 30 seconds,

then peel them. In a frying pan, fry the courgette, tomato, garlic and lemon over a high heat. Stir thoroughly and remove from the heat. Place the chicken and vegetables onto four rectangles of greaseproof paper, make up the parcels and seal them up. Bake in the oven for 15–20 minutes.

POULE CITRONNÉE, SAUCE CURRY ET GINGEMBRE (CHICKEN WITH A LEMON AND GINGER SAUCE)

(4 servings)

Preparation time: 30 minutes
Cooking time: 1 hour 5 minutes

1 whole chicken
1 bouquet garni
1 teaspoon herbes de Provence (mixed herbs)
2 bay leaves
1 low-salt chicken stock cube
1 red pepper, cut into thin strips
Salt and black pepper
5–6 carrots
3 drops of oil
1 onion, thinly sliced
1 pinch of curry powder
1 tablespoon cornflour
1 lemon, cut into quarters
1 teaspoon very thinly sliced ginger

Fill a casserole dish three-quarters full with water and add to it the chicken, bouquet garni, herbs, bay leaf, stock cube, pepper, salt and black pepper. Bring to the boil, cover and cook for about 50 minutes over a gentle heat. Add the carrots and continue cooking for 10 minutes. In a high-sided, non-stick frying pan (oiled and wiped with kitchen paper) sweat the onion with the curry powder, the cornflour mixed with a little cold water, the lemon and ginger. Drain the chicken and remove the skin, then cut it up into pieces. Add the chicken to the sauce and adjust the seasoning. Serve the carrots separately.

POULET À L'ESTRAGON ET AUX GIROLLES (CHICKEN WITH CHANTERELLE MUSHROOMS)

(4–6 servings)

Preparation time: 20 minutes
Cooking time: 35 minutes

6 chicken legs
Salt and black pepper
3 drops of oil
100ml (3½fl oz) low-salt chicken stock
1 sprig of tarragon
1kg (2¼lb) chanterelle mushrooms, cleaned
1 garlic clove, very finely chopped
1 bunch of parsley, very finely chopped
250g (9oz) virtually fat-free fromage frais

Brown the chicken legs, seasoned with salt and pepper, in a casserole dish (oiled and wiped with kitchen paper). Add the stock and the tarragon sprig. Bring to the boil, cover, lower the heat, then cook for 25 minutes. In a frying pan, gently fry the chanterelle mushrooms with the garlic and parsley. Season. When the chicken is ready to be served, remove the tarragon from the casserole dish and deglaze the sauce with the fromage frais over a gentle heat. Adjust the seasoning. Serve the chicken hot with the fried chanterelle mushrooms.

POULET AUX AROMATES
(ROAST HERBY CHICKEN)

(4 servings)

Preparation time: 15 minutes (plus leaving overnight)
Cooking time: 1 hour 30 minutes

1 whole chicken
1 bunch of basil
3 garlic cloves
1 lemon, cut into quarters
A few sprigs of thyme
A few sprigs of rosemary
200g (7oz) leeks, finely chopped
250g (9oz) carrots, finely chopped
Salt and black pepper

Preheat the oven to 220°C/425°C/Gas 7.

Stuff the chicken with the basil, garlic, lemon quarters, thyme and rosemary. Leave overnight in the fridge for the flavours to develop. The following day, put the leek and carrot into a deep roasting tin and season with salt and pepper. Pour a little water over them, place the chicken on top and roast for 1 hour to 1 hour 30 minutes. Serve piping hot, with the skin taken off the chicken.

POULET AUX CHAMPIGNONS (CHICKEN WITH MUSHROOMS)

(4 servings)

Preparation time: 20 minutes
Cooking time: 30 minutes

600g (1¼lb) button mushrooms
1 lemon
Salt and black pepper
1 onion, chopped
800g (1lb 12oz) chicken breasts, cut into cubes
2 tomatoes, chopped
2 garlic cloves, chopped
250ml (9fl oz) low-salt chicken stock

Chop the ends off the mushroom stalks and thinly slice the mushrooms, then sprinkle a few drops of lemon juice over them to prevent them from turning black. Put the mushrooms in a non-stick casserole dish. Season with salt and pepper, cover and cook over a gentle heat until all their water has evaporated. Drain them and put to one side. Brown the onion in a casserole dish in a little water. Add the chicken, tomato, mushroom, garlic, chicken stock, salt and pepper. Cover and cook over a gentle heat for 20 minutes.

POULET AUX POIVRONS
(STIR-FRIED CHICKEN WITH PEPPERS AND BAMBOO SHOOTS)

(4 servings)

Preparation time: 40 minutes (plus 2 hours marinating)
Cooking time: 30 minutes

4 chicken breasts, cut into strips
2 tablespoons soy sauce
2 teaspoons grated ginger
1 garlic clove, thinly sliced
2 sprigs of mint, very finely chopped
2 sprigs of coriander, very finely chopped
1 green pepper
1 red pepper
3 drops of oil
1 onion, thinly sliced
140g (5oz) bamboo shoots, rinsed and cut smaller
Salt and black pepper

Place the chicken strips in a shallow dish and pour the soy sauce and ginger over them. Add the garlic, mint and coriander. Cover with clingfilm and marinate for 2 hours in the fridge. Drain the chicken, sieve the marinade and put to one side. Grill the peppers for 10–15 minutes until charred all over. Place in a plastic bag and leave to cool, before peeling away the skin and seeds and cutting into strips. In a non-stick frying pan (oiled and wiped with kitchen paper), brown the chicken for 5 minutes and fry the onion until golden brown. Add the peppers and continue cooking for 4 minutes, then pour in the marinade and cook for 3 more minutes. Stir in the bamboo shoots and heat for a further minute. Season to taste before serving.

POULET BASQUAISE (BASQUE CHICKEN)

(4 servings)

Preparation time: 15 minutes
Cooking time: 1 hour 5 minutes

1kg (2¼lb) tomatoes
1 whole chicken, cut into pieces
Salt and black pepper
3 drops of oil
1 carrot, peeled and cut into small pieces
2 peppers, diced
2 garlic cloves, chopped
1 bouquet garni

Poach the tomatoes in boiling water for 30 seconds, then peel and deseed them. Season the chicken and brown in a non-stick casserole dish (oiled and wiped with kitchen paper) over a medium heat. Add the tomatoes, carrot, pepper, garlic and bouquet garni. Season with salt and pepper. Cover and cook for 1 hour over a very gentle heat. Serve the chicken with the skin removed.

POULET MARENGO
(CHICKEN MARENGO)

(4 servings)

Preparation time: 30 minutes
Cooking time: 1 hour

1 whole chicken, cut into pieces
Salt and black pepper
2 onions, sliced
2 shallots, sliced
1 garlic clove, sliced
2 tablespoons white wine vinegar
1 tablespoon tomato purée
4 tomatoes, diced
A few sprigs of thyme
1 small bay leaf sprig
3 parsley stalks

Brown the chicken pieces, seasoned with salt and pepper, over a high heat in a non-stick casserole dish (oiled and wiped with kitchen paper), then remove the pieces from the dish. In their place, add the onion, shallot and garlic and fry them over a medium heat for 2 minutes. Moisten with 200ml (7fl oz) water, the vinegar and tomato purée. Add the tomato. Transfer the chicken pieces back to the casserole dish and season with salt and pepper. Add the thyme, bay leaf and parsley, cover and simmer for 45 minutes. Serve the chicken with the skin removed.

POULET POCHÉ, SAUCE LÉGÈRE AUX HERBES FRAÎCHES (POACHED CHICKEN IN A LIGHT HERB SAUCE)

(4 servings)

Preparation time: 30 minutes
Cooking time: 1 hour

½ lemon
1 whole chicken
1 onion, cut in half and studded with a clove
1 carrot, quartered
2 leeks, tied together with a celery stick
1 bouquet garni
1 garlic clove, cut in half
Salt

For the sauce
2 egg yolks
25g (1oz) virtually fat-free fromage frais
1 teaspoon chopped herbs (chives, tarragon, parsley, chervil)

Rub the half lemon all over the surface of the chicken, then place the chicken in a casserole dish. Add the vegetables, bouquet garni and garlic. Pour in cold water to about 2cm (¾ inch) above the chicken and add a pinch of salt. Bring to the boil, skim off any foam, and cook over a gentle heat for 40–45 minutes. Once cooked, drain the chicken and take 150ml (5fl oz) of the chicken stock, skim off any fat and keep it warm. Put the egg yolks in a bowl and add 1 tablespoon cold water. Heat this sauce in a *bain-marie* or by placing the bowl over a pan of simmering water. Beat the eggs until creamy, taking care not to overheat them. Whisk in the fromage frais, then pour the warm stock into the sauce, stirring continuously. Add the herbs and adjust the seasoning. Serve piping hot with the skinned chicken.

SALADE AU YAOURT AUX HERBES
(YOGHURT AND HERB CHICKEN SALAD)

(2 servings)

Preparation time: 15 minutes
No cooking required

150g (5½oz) fat-free natural yoghurt
1 garlic clove, chopped
1 teaspoon mustard
A few sprigs of parsley, chopped
A few chives, finely chopped
Salt and black pepper
300g (10½oz) button mushrooms, cut into small cubes
1 bunch of radishes, cut into small cubes
4 slices cooked chicken with herbs, diced
4 large continental gherkins, cut into thick slices

Prepare the sauce by mixing together the yoghurt with the garlic, mustard, parsley, chives, salt and pepper. Pour into a dish and keep in a cool place before serving over the vegetables, chicken and gherkins.

POULET PROVENÇAL
(PROVENÇAL CHICKEN)

(4 servings)

Preparation time: 15 minutes
Cooking time: 1 hour

1 whole chicken, cut into pieces
1 tin of chopped tomatoes
4 garlic cloves, crushed
1 small bunch of parsley, finely chopped
Salt and black pepper

Brown the chicken in a non-stick, high-sided frying pan. Put to one side. Next put the chopped tomatoes, garlic, parsley, salt and pepper into the frying pan. Place over a moderate heat, cover and cook for 30 minutes. Return the chicken pieces to the pan with a little water, if necessary. Cover and continue cooking for 20 minutes. Serve the chicken with the skin removed.

TERRINE DE POULET À L'ESTRAGON
(TARRAGON CHICKEN TERRINE)

(6 servings)

Preparation time: 40 minutes (plus 24 hours
  refrigeration)
Cooking time: 1 hour 30 minutes

1 whole chicken, trussed and tied
500ml (18fl oz) low-salt strong chicken stock
2 leeks, cleaned
3 carrots, peeled
2 garlic cloves, peeled
1 onion, peeled
1 bunch of tarragon
Salt and black pepper
200g (7oz) chicken livers
2 gelatine leaves

Prepare this recipe a day ahead. Place the chicken
in a casserole dish, pour in the stock and cover with
cold water. Add the leeks, carrots, garlic and onion,
a few sprigs of tarragon and some salt and pepper.
Bring to the boil, cover and cook for 1 hour 30 minutes
over a gentle heat, skimming the top at regular
intervals. After 45 minutes, add the trimmed chicken
livers. Once cooked, dice up the chicken, chicken
livers, carrots and leeks separately into large cubes.
Reduce the stock to half its quantity and strain. Add

the gelatine leaves that have been soaking in a bowl of cold water for a few minutes. Line the bottom of a terrine dish with tarragon leaves and pour in a little of the stock. Build up successive layers, adding first half the chicken, then the chicken livers, carrots and the rest of the vegetables. Cover with the stock and refrigerate for 24 hours.

BROCHETTES DE POULET MARINE (CHICKEN AND PEPPER KEBABS)

(4 servings)

Preparation time: 30 minutes (plus overnight marinating)
Cooking time: 10 minutes

You will need kebab sticks (soak in a little water if using wooden sticks so that they do not burn when the meat is being cooked).

4 chicken breasts
4 garlic cloves, chopped
Juice of 2 lemons
1 teaspoon ground cumin
1 teaspoon thyme
Salt and black pepper
1 green pepper (or red, depending on your
    preference), cut into cubes
8 shallots, quartered

The day before, cut the chicken breasts into pieces and place in a shallow dish with the garlic, lemon juice, cumin, thyme and some salt and black pepper. Cover with clingfilm and leave to marinate overnight in a cool place. Make up the kebabs by alternating the chicken and vegetables, brush with the marinade and cook on the barbecue or under the grill for 5 minutes on each side.

ROULADE DE JAMBON AUX FINES HERBES (HERBY CHICKEN ROULADE)

(2 servings)

Preparation time: 15 minutes
Cooking time: 10 minutes

1 egg
50g (1¾oz) pink radishes, chopped
2 shallots, chopped
50g (1¾oz) cucumber, chopped
3–4 chives, chopped
3 sprigs of parsley, chopped
1 pinch of tarragon, chopped
250g (9oz) virtually fat-free fromage frais
Salt and black pepper
4 slices of cooked chicken
1 tomato
4 cornichons (small gherkins)

Cook the egg for 10 minutes in boiling water until hard-boiled. Mix the radish with the shallot, cucumber, herbs and fromage frais and season with salt and pepper. Spread this mixture over the chicken slices and roll them up. Serve with half a tomato, hard-boiled egg and a couple of gherkins each.

TERRINE DE VOLAILLE
(CHICKEN AND PINK PEPPERCORN TERRINE)

Preparation time: 45 minutes (plus chilling time)
Cooking time: 1 hour

2 carrots
1 leek
1 onion
1 whole chicken, weighing around 1.5kg (3lb 5oz), cut into pieces
Salt and black pepper
2 tomatoes
1 sprig of tarragon
1 egg white
1 teaspoon pink peppercorns

Peel the vegetables and place them (except for the tomatoes) in a stockpot with 1 litre (1¾ pints) water. Bring to the boil. Add the chicken, salt and pepper and skim off any foam, then leave to boil away gently, uncovered, for 1 hour. Remove the chicken, let it drain, then take off all the meat and chop it up finely. Deseed the tomatoes and cut into chunks. Place the chicken pieces in a cake tin and layer them with the tomato chunks and tarragon leaves. Bring the stock to the boil again, then reduce it to around 250ml (9fl oz). Beat the egg white until stiff, put it into the stock and boil for 1 minute. Allow to cool, and then strain through some muslin. Next pour this over the chicken and sprinkle the pink peppercorns on top. Arrange a few pieces of tomato and about 10 tarragon leaves evenly over the top of the terrine. A few hours later, turn the terrine out onto a dish and keep it in the fridge to be served cold.

TERRINE ESTIVALE
(SUMMER TERRINE)
(8 servings)

Preparation time: 30 minutes (plus 4 hours refrigeration)
Cooking time: 1 hour 30 minutes

1kg (2¼lb) French beans
500ml (18fl oz) low-salt stock
1 carrot
1 stick of celery
1 onion
5 sprigs of tarragon, chopped
½ teaspoon oregano, chopped

8 slices of extra-lean ham (or cooked turkey or
    chicken)
4 eggs
300g (10½oz) virtually fat-free fromage frais
1 tablespoon extra-light cream cheese (optional)
Salt and black pepper

Preheat the oven to 180°C/350°F/Gas 4.
Cook the French beans in the stock, uncovered, for 15
minutes. Drain the beans, then cut them into smaller
pieces. Chop the carrot, celery and onion together in
a food processor or blender. In a non-stick, high-sided
frying pan, fry this chopped mixture over a gentle heat
for 10 minutes. Add the beans to the frying pan and
cook over a gentle heat, stirring from time to time,
until the beans no longer give off any water. Add the
tarragon and oregano. Line a 2 litre (3½ pint) cake tin
with greaseproof paper, allowing the paper to overlap
the longest sides of the tin. Line the tin with six slices
of ham, allowing those slices to overlap. Spoon in the
vegetables. In a bowl, beat together the eggs, fromage
frais and cream cheese. Season with salt and pepper,
then gently pour this mixture over the vegetables.
Fold over the ham, cover with the remaining ham and
finally cover with a sheet of aluminium foil. Place the
tin into a bigger dish and fill this *bain-marie* half full
with cold water. Bake for 1 hour. Leave to cool, then
refrigerate for 4 hours.

COQUELETS AU CITRON ET AUX TOMATES CERISES (ROAST LEMON POUSSIN WITH CHERRY TOMATOES)

(2 servings)

Preparation time: 20 minutes
Cooking time: 40 minutes

2 poussins
5 sprigs of thyme
1 lemon, cut into slices
500ml (18fl oz) chicken stock
2 medium onions, thinly sliced
700g (1lb 9oz) cherry tomatoes
2 garlic cloves, chopped
Salt and black pepper

Preheat the oven to 180°C/350°F/Gas 4.
Place the poussins in a baking dish, remove the thyme leaves from the sprigs and scatter them over the birds. Cover them with the lemon slices. Bake in the oven for 20 minutes. After 10 minutes, moisten with the chicken stock. Take the dish out of the oven and arrange the onion, tomatoes and garlic around the poussins. Season with salt and pepper and mix together so that the tomatoes are coated with cooking juices. Return to the oven for 20 minutes. Remove the skin from the poussin before eating.

BLANC DE POIREAU BACON
(LEEK AND TURKEY BAKE)

(4 servings)

Preparation time: 20 minutes
Cooking time: 35 minutes

800g (1¾lb) leeks (white part only), cut into small
   pieces
200g (7oz) cooked turkey slices
1 shallot, very finely chopped
2 eggs
90g (3oz) virtually fat-free fromage frais
Salt
3 drops of oil

Preheat the oven to 190°C/375°F/Gas 5.
Steam the leek in a pressure cooker or steamer for
10 minutes. In a frying pan, brown the turkey slices
with the shallot. Whisk together the eggs with the
fromage frais and salt. Stir the turkey and shallot into
the leek and put into a baking dish (oiled and wiped
with kitchen paper). Pour the egg and fromage frais
mixture over the leek and bake for 20 minutes.

CUISSES DE DINDE AUX POIVRONS
(TURKEY DRUMSTICKS WITH RED PEPPERS)

(2 servings)

Preparation time: 30 minutes
Cooking time: 50 minutes

2 turkey drumsticks
3 red peppers
50ml (2fl oz) wine vinegar
2 tablespoons virtually fat-free fromage frais
Salt and black pepper

Brown the turkey drumsticks in a non-stick casserole dish with a little water. Cover and cook for 40 minutes over a gentle heat, turning them over regularly. Grill the peppers for 10 to 15 minutes until charred all over. Place in a plastic bag and leave to cool, before peeling away the skin and seeds. Cut them up and whiz them in a blender to produce a purée. Remove the drumsticks from the dish and keep warm. Deglaze the dish with some vinegar. Stir together the fromage frais, pepper purée, salt and pepper, add to the dish and bring to the boil. Arrange the drumsticks on a dish and cover them with the pepper sauce.

PAUPIETTES DE DINDE
(TURKEY OLIVES)

(4 servings)

Preparation time: 30 minutes
Cooking time: 1 hour 10 minutes

100g (3½oz) button mushrooms
1 onion
Parsley
Salt and black pepper
4 slices of extra-lean ham
4 turkey escalopes
500ml (18fl oz) low-salt stock

Chop up the mushroom stalks with half of the onion and some parsley. Fry for 5–6 minutes over a medium heat in a non-stick frying pan, without any fat. Season with salt and pepper. Place a slice of ham onto each escalope and then add the mushroom purée. Roll it all up and tie together with string. Brown the rolled turkey olives in the frying pan over a medium heat, then place in a casserole dish. Roughly chop up the rest of the onion. Add to the dish with the stock and 250ml (9fl oz) water and season with salt and pepper. Cover and simmer over a gentle heat for 45 minutes. Add the mushroom tops and cook for a further 20 minutes. Serve immediately.

PINTADE AU CHOU
(GUINEA FOWL WITH SAVOY CABBAGE)

(4 servings)

Preparation time: 30 minutes
Cooking time: 1 hour 25 minutes

½ lemon
1 guinea fowl
1 Savoy cabbage, cut into 8 pieces
1 onion, with a clove inserted
1 bouquet garni
Salt and black pepper
1 tablespoon bilberries or blueberries
500ml (18fl oz) low-salt chicken stock

Preheat the oven to 220°C/425°C/Gas 7.
Rub the lemon over the guinea fowl and place it under a grill. Brown it for 5 minutes. In the meantime, prepare the cabbage by blanching it for 5 minutes in salted boiling water, then draining. Put the guinea fowl in a casserole dish and place the cabbage all around it. Add the onion, bouquet garni, black pepper and bilberries and moisten with the stock. Cover and bake for 1 hour 15 minutes, basting the guinea fowl regularly. Once the bird is cooked, reduce the stock as much as possible, check the seasoning and remove the skin from the guinea fowl before serving.

Meat and vegetables

BOEUF À LA FICELLE
(BEEF ON A STRING)

(1 serving)

Preparation time: 20 minutes
Cooking time: 35 minutes

1 bouquet garni
½ onion
1 clove
70g (2½oz) carrots, roughly chopped
1 leek (white part only), roughly chopped
70g (2½oz) celery, roughly chopped
Salt and black pepper
250g (9oz) fillet of beef

Pour 1 litre (1¾ pints) water into a casserole dish. Add the bouquet garni, the onion studded with the clove and the vegetables. Season and bring everything to the boil. Tie a piece of string around the beef and drop it into this simmering bouillon. Cover and cook over a medium heat for about 30 minutes. Take the meat out, cut it into pieces and arrange on a serving dish with the vegetables all around it as an accompaniment.

BŒUF AUX AUBERGINES
(BEEF WITH AUBERGINES)
(4 servings)

Preparation time: 15 minutes
Cooking time: 50 minutes

300g (10½oz) aubergines, peeled and cut into thin
  slices
1 garlic clove, finely chopped
1 tablespoon parsley, chopped
400g (14oz) medium tomatoes, quartered
500g (1lb 2oz) lean beef, cut into thin strips
Salt and black pepper

Preheat the oven to 220°C/425°F/Gas 7.
Sprinkle the aubergine with a little salt and leave to degorge any juices for 15 minutes. Scatter the garlic and parsley over the tomatoes, bring to the boil in a casserole dish and then simmer for 30 minutes over a medium heat. Put half the aubergine and tomato in the bottom of a small baking dish and season. Place the meat on top. Cover with the rest of the aubergine and tomato and bake for 15 minutes.

BŒUF AUX POIVRONS
(BEEF AND RED PEPPERS)

(4 servings)

Preparation time: 20 minutes (plus 2 hours marinating)
Cooking time: 1 hour

325g (11½oz) sirloin steak, cut into very thin strips
4 small red peppers, thinly sliced
3 small onions, thinly sliced
3 drops of oil
2 tablespoons soy sauce
Salt and black pepper

For the marinade
1 teaspoon cornflour
4 tablespoons soy sauce

Prepare the marinade, add the beef and keep in a cool place for 2 hours. Put the pepper and onion into a casserole dish (oiled and wiped with kitchen paper) and gently fry. Add a cup of water and cook over a very gentle heat for 30 minutes. Once cooked, add the marinated meat, the 2 tablespoons soy sauce and a little water, if necessary. Cook the beef for 30 minutes and season according to taste.

BOEUF BOURGUIGNON (BEEF BOURGUIGNON)

(6 servings)

Preparation time: 10 minutes
Cooking time: 2 hours 30 minutes

500g (1lb 2oz) lean beef, cut into cubes
3 drops of oil
1 low-salt beef stock cube
1 teaspoon cornflour
1 teaspoon parsley, chopped
1 garlic clove, finely chopped
1 bay leaf
Salt and black pepper
3 medium onions, finely chopped
150g (5½oz) button mushrooms, sliced

Preheat the oven to 200°C/400°F/Gas 6.
Brown the beef in a large frying pan (oiled and wiped with kitchen paper), then put the meat in a casserole dish. Dissolve the beef stock cube in 250ml (9fl oz) boiling water and pour into the frying pan with the cornflour, parsley, garlic, bay leaf and seasoning. Bring to the boil and allow to thicken slightly. Pour this over the beef (add some water if the sauce does not cover the meat), cover and bake for 2 hours. Fry the onion and mushroom in the frying pan over a medium heat and add them to the meat during the last 30 minutes of cooking.

STEAK À LA MEXICAINE
(MEXICAN STEAK)

(1 serving)
Preparation time: 20 minutes
Cooking time: 10 minutes

250g (9oz) minced beef
Salt and black pepper
2 pinches of Mexican spice mixture
3 drops of oil
2 medium tomatoes

Mix together the minced beef, salt, pepper and half the spice mixture and make up small meatballs. Cook in a frying pan (oiled and wiped with kitchen paper) over a high heat, without letting them dry out. Poach the tomatoes in boiling water for 30 seconds, then peel and finely chop. In another frying pan, cook the tomato with the remaining Mexican spice mixture over a gentle heat until the sauce is smooth, then pour it over the meatballs and serve straight away.

FRICHTI VIANDE ET COURGETTES (BEEF AND COURGETTE RAGOUT)

(4 servings)

Preparation time: 20 minutes
Cooking time: 45 minutes

You will need a steamer.

1kg (2¼lb) courgettes, sliced
500g (1lb 2oz) lean minced beef
3 drops of oil
400g (14oz) tomato passata
1 garlic clove
3 stalks of parsley
Salt and black pepper

Steam the courgette for 20 minutes. In the meantime, brown the meat for 10 minutes in a non-stick frying pan (oiled and wiped with kitchen paper). Add the tomato passata, garlic, parsley and salt and pepper. Cook for 15 more minutes. Stir everything together well to serve.

STEAK CHOPPED À LA HONGROISE (HUNGARIAN MINCED STEAK)

(4 servings)

Preparation time: 15 minutes
Cooking time: 20 minutes

6 small shallots, chopped
1 red pepper, deseeded and diced
3 drops of oil
500g (1lb 2oz) lean minced beef (5% fat)
2 tablespoons paprika
100ml (3½fl oz) tomato passata
Salt and black pepper
1 pinch of cayenne pepper
½ lemon
85g (3oz) virtually fat-free fromage frais

Fry the shallot and pepper in a frying pan (oiled and wiped with kitchen paper) over a low heat for 5 minutes. Remove the vegetables from the frying pan, then use it to cook the minced beef for 5 minutes over a high heat, crushing it with a fork. Add the paprika, tomato passata and fried shallot and pepper. Cook for another 5 minutes, stirring well, and season with salt, pepper and cayenne pepper. Squeeze the half lemon and whisk it into the fromage frais. Stir this into the mince, away from the heat, then warm the sauce through again without allowing it to boil.

BOEUF SAUTÉ AUX LÉGUMES
(SAUTÉED BEEF WITH VEGETABLES)

(4 servings)

Preparation time: 30 minutes (plus 30 minutes
   marinating)
Cooking time: 5 minutes

500g (1lb 2oz) tender beef, sliced
6 tablespoons soy sauce
1 tablespoon sherry vinegar
1 tablespoon cornflour
3 drops of oil
1 bunch of spring onions, thinly sliced lengthways
1 green pepper, deseeded and cut into thin strips
2 carrots, cut into medium-sized slices
1 teaspoon liquid sweetener
Salt and black pepper

Put the beef slices into a dish with the soy sauce,
sherry vinegar and cornflour. Mix together and leave
to marinate for 30 minutes in a cool place. Drain the
meat and brown in a non-stick high-sided frying pan
(oiled and wiped with kitchen paper) for 1 minute over
a high heat. Keep warm while you fry the vegetables
for 3 minutes in the frying pan. Add the marinade and
beef, pour over the sweetener and add salt and black
pepper. Heat it all through over a medium heat for 1
minute, stirring all the time. Serve immediately.

BROCHETTE DE BOEUF TURGLOFF
(TURGLOFF BEEF KEBABS)

(2 servings)

Preparation time: 20 minutes
Cooking time: 25 minutes

You will need kebab sticks (soak in a little water if using wooden sticks so that they do not burn when the meat is being cooked).

500g (1lb 2oz) tomatoes
1 garlic clove, crushed
Salt and black pepper
600g (1¼lb) lean beef, cut into chunks
200g (7oz) peppers, cut into chunks
200g (7oz) onions, cut into chunks
Juice of 1 lemon
Celery salt
Parsley

Poach the tomatoes in boiling water for 30 seconds, then peel and deseed them and crush. Simmer the tomato with the garlic in a frying pan. Season. Thread the beef, pepper and onion onto the kebab sticks and grill for about 10 minutes, either on the barbecue or under the grill. When ready to serve, remove the ingredients from the sticks onto two plates, sprinkle with lemon juice and add some celery salt. Pour a little of the tomato sauce onto each plate and garnish with the parsley.

ROULEAUX D'OMELETTE AU BOEUF
(BEEF OMELETTE ROLLS)

(4 servings)

Preparation time: 30 minutes (plus at least 3 hours marinating)
Cooking time: 15 minutes

700g (1lb 9oz) fillet of beef, thinly sliced
2 tablespoons soy sauce
2 garlic cloves, crushed
1 teaspoon grated ginger
3 drops of oil
10 eggs
Salt and black pepper
1 large onion, finely chopped
1 carrot, finely chopped
125g (4½oz) soya bean sprouts
6 chives, chopped

Mix the beef together with half the soy sauce, the garlic and ginger. Cover and leave to marinate in a cool place for at least 3 hours or overnight. In a frying pan (oiled and wiped with kitchen paper), cook eight thin omelettes from the eggs beaten with 4 tablespoons water and some seasoning. Keep warm. Fry the beef and onion over a medium heat in the frying pan until the meat is golden brown. Add the rest of the soy sauce and cook until it starts to boil. Stir in the carrot and sauté until tender. Add the soya bean sprouts and chives, stirring together well. Divide this mixture among the omelettes, roll them up and then cut them in half.

PAIN DE VIANDE AUX CHAMPIGNONS (MEAT LOAF WITH MUSHROOMS)

(2 servings)

Preparation time: 20 minutes
Cooking time: 55 minutes

2 eggs
400g (14oz) lean beef mince
400g (14oz) lean veal mince
1 onion, finely chopped
2 garlic cloves, crushed
Salt and black pepper
A few sprigs of thyme, rosemary and parsley
150g (5½oz) button mushrooms, very finely chopped
3 drops of oil

Preheat the oven to 240°C/475°F/Gas 9.
Stir the eggs into the beef and veal with the onion and garlic. Season with salt and pepper. Blend the herbs and add them. Gently sweat the mushrooms in a non-stick saucepan (oiled and wiped with kitchen paper), then add to the minced meat mixture. Pour into a cake tin. Bake in the oven at for 45–50 minutes. Can be eaten either hot or cold.

HACHIS AU CHOU DE BRUXELLES (CAULIFLOWER SHEPHERD'S PIE)

(6 servings)

Preparation time: 20 minutes
Cooking time: 1 hour

You will need a steamer.

1.25kg (2lb 12oz) cauliflower
600g (1¼lb) minced beef
1 onion
2 garlic cloves
1 small bunch of parsley
Salt and black pepper

Preheat the oven to 180°C/350°F/Gas 4.
Steam the cauliflower florets for 15 minutes. Whiz in a blender to produce a purée. Next, blend the beef, onion, garlic, parsley, salt and pepper. Spread the mixture out evenly in a baking dish, then put the cauliflower purée over it and bake for 45 minutes.

RAGOÛT DE BOEUF AUX DEUX POIVRONS (TWO PEPPER BEEF STEW)

(4 servings)

Preparation time: 20 minutes
Cooking time: 50 minutes

450g (1lb) diced beef
½ onion, chopped
1 garlic clove, chopped
1 tablespoon tomato purée
500ml (18fl oz) low-salt beef stock
Salt and black pepper
1 green pepper, deseeded and cut into strips
1 red pepper, deseeded and cut into strips
1 carrot, chopped
1 turnip, chopped
1 tablespoon potato flour
2 tablespoons water

In a saucepan, sear the beef over a high heat. Add the onion and garlic and continue cooking for 1 minute, stirring continuously. Add the tomato purée and the stock and season with salt and pepper. Bring to the boil, cover and simmer for 20 minutes over a gentle heat. Add the chopped vegetables to the saucepan and cook for a further 10 minutes. Mix the potato flour with 2 tablespoons water, add to the pan and continue cooking for 3 minutes, stirring from time to time.

FEUILLETÉ D'AUBERGINES À LA CRÉTOISE (CRETAN MOUSSAKA)

(2 servings)

Preparation time: 20 minutes
Cooking time: 35 minutes

600g (1¼lb) minced beef
2 garlic cloves, crushed
15 mint leaves, very finely chopped
400g (14oz) tomato passata
2 aubergines, cut lengthways into several 1cm (½ inch) thick slices
3 drops of oil
200g (7oz) fat-free natural yoghurt
Salt and black pepper

Preheat the oven to 200°C/400°F/Gas 6.
Fry the meat in a large non-stick frying pan and add the garlic, mint and tomato passata. Cover and simmer for 20 minutes, stirring from time to time. Gently fry the aubergine in another frying pan (oiled and wiped with kitchen paper) for 3 minutes on both sides over a medium heat, then place them on kitchen paper. Pour the yoghurt over the meat, stir and season. Take a small gratin dish and arrange in it, side-by-side, two slices of aubergine. Cover them with the meat sauce, then continue building up alternate layers, finishing off with a layer of aubergines. Bake for 5 minutes and serve.

ÉMINCÉ DE BOEUF AU VINAIGRE ET COURGETTES (THINLY SLICED BEEF WITH RASPBERRY VINEGAR AND COURGETTES)

(4 servings)

Preparation time: 1 hour
Cooking time: 45 minutes

3 garlic cloves, chopped
1 onion, chopped
4 courgettes, cut into strips
3 drops of oil
600g (1¼lb) lean beef, cut into small, thin, even-sized
   pieces
100ml (3½fl oz) raspberry vinegar
2 sprigs of parsley, chopped
¼ bunch of tarragon, chopped
Salt and black pepper

Fry the garlic, onion and courgette in a non-stick frying pan (oiled and wiped with kitchen paper). Stir well so that the vegetables brown on all sides. Pour in a cup of water, cover, and cook over a gentle heat for 20 minutes. Put to one side. In the same frying pan, sear the meat over a high heat for 5 minutes and add the vinegar. Mix together before returning the vegetables to the frying pan. Simmer for 15 minutes and, at the last moment, add the parsley and tarragon. Season with salt and pepper and serve piping hot.

COURGETTES FARCIES
(SPICY STUFFED COURGETTES)

(4 servings)

Preparation time: 10 minutes
Cooking time: 35 minutes

4 courgettes, halved lengthways and deseeded
Salt and black pepper
500g (1lb 2oz) lean minced beef
1 jar or tin of salsa verde (a Mexican sauce made from
    green tomatoes and chillies)
200g (7oz) virtually fat-free fromage frais

Preheat the oven to 240°C/475°F/Gas 9.
Season the courgette with salt and pepper. Brown
the minced beef in a non-stick frying pan, then mix
together with the salsa verde and fromage frais. Fill
the courgettes with this stuffing mixture and bake for
30 minutes.

ESCALOPES DE VEAU AUX CAROTTES RÂPÉES CITRONNÉES (VEAL ESCALOPES WITH LEMONY GRATED CARROTS)

(4 servings)

Preparation time: 15 minutes
Cooking time: 20 minutes

500g (1lb 2oz) carrots
3 drops of oil
Grated zest and juice of 1 lemon
4 thin veal escalopes

Blanch the carrots in a saucepan of boiling water, then drain. Roughly grate the carrots and in a frying pan (oiled and wiped with kitchen paper), gently fry with the lemon zest, covered with a sheet of greaseproof paper. Remove the greaseproof paper and add the lemon juice. Brown the veal escalopes in another non-stick frying pan (oiled and wiped with kitchen paper) over a gentle heat for 7–8 minutes, then add the carrots and the cooking juices and allow to reduce a little.

FILETS DE VEAU EN PAPILLOTE
(OVEN-BAKED VEAL PARCELS)

(4 servings)

Preparation time: 15 minutes
Cooking time: 25 minutes

1 onion, thinly sliced
1 carrot, thinly sliced
1 leek (white part only), thinly sliced
Salt and black pepper
4 tablespoons of chopped herbs (parsley, thyme, chives)
4 veal fillets, each weighing 125g (4½oz)

Preheat the oven to 180°C/350°F/Gas 4.
Gently brown the vegetables in a saucepan, adding 2 tablespoons water and some seasoning. Cover and cook for 6 minutes. Cut out four squares of aluminium foil and in the centre arrange the vegetables, herbs and veal fillets. Seal up the parcels and bake for 10 minutes.

JARRET DE VEAU À LA NIÇOISE
(SHIN OF VEAL NIÇOISE)

(4 servings)

Preparation time: 30 minutes
Cooking time: 1 hour 50 minutes

750g (1lb 10oz) firm tomatoes
2 medium carrots, sliced
2 medium onions, sliced
1 garlic clove, chopped
½ lemon, cut into four
1 bouquet garni
1 shin of veal, 700g (1lb 9oz), sliced
Salt and black pepper
1 level tablespoon tomato purée

Poach the tomatoes in boiling water for 30 seconds, then peel and deseed them. Cut into large pieces. Place the carrot and onion in a casserole dish, pour over a cup of water and bring to the boil. Add the tomato, garlic, lemon pieces and bouquet garni. Bring back to the boil and stir everything together carefully. Add the veal slices and season with salt and pepper. Cover and cook over a gentle heat for 1 hour 30 minutes to 1 hour 45 minutes. Once cooked, remove the bouquet garni, add the tomato purée and adjust the seasoning. Take out the slices of veal, arrange them on a serving dish and cover with the vegetables and sauce.

OSSO BUCCO
(OSSO BUCCO)
(4 servings)

Preparation time: 15 minutes
Cooking time: 1 hour 40 minutes

1 shin of veal, 1kg (2¼lb), sliced
1kg (2¼lb) carrots, sliced
Zest and juice of 1 lemon
Zest of 1 orange
8 level teaspoons tomato purée
1 pinch of oregano
Salt and black pepper

Brown the veal slices for 7–8 minutes under the grill. Put the carrot in a casserole dish. Sprinkle over the lemon juice and add the lemon and orange zest. Dilute the tomato purée in 500ml (18fl oz) hot water and pour it over the carrots. Add the oregano, salt and pepper and simmer over a medium heat. Place the veal slices in the casserole dish. Cover and cook over a gentle heat for about 1 hour 30 minutes.

PAIN DE VEAU AU YAOURT
(VEAL MEAT LOAF)

(2 servings)

Preparation time: 10 minutes
Cooking time: 1 hour

750g (1lb 10oz) minced veal
400g (14 oz) carrots, grated
1 onion, chopped
1 garlic clove, chopped
200g (7oz) mushrooms, sliced
300g (10½oz) fat-free natural yoghurt

Preheat the oven to 180°C/350°F/Gas 4.
Mix together all the ingredients and put in an ovenproof tin. Bake in the oven for 1 hour. This veal loaf is delicious eaten hot or cold.

PAUPIETTES DE VEAU JONQUILLE
(JONQUILLE'S VEAL OLIVES)

(2 servings)

Preparation time: 20 minutes
Cooking time: 1 hour 10 minutes

2 eggs
2 x 100g (3 ½oz) veal escalopes
Salt and black pepper
100g (3½oz) onions, finely chopped
100g (3½oz) button mushrooms, finely chopped
A few sprigs of thyme
1 small bay leaf
500ml (18fl oz) tomato juice

Preheat the oven to 190°C/375°F/Gas 5.
Cook the eggs for 10 minutes in boiling water until hard-boiled. Roll each hard-boiled egg up inside one wide, flat escalope. Sprinkle salt inside and then carefully tie up the olives with some string. Place them in a small baking dish and add the onion, mushroom, thyme and bay leaf. Season the tomato juice and pour it over. Cover and bake for about 1 hour. Take the olives out and remove the string. Cut the olives in two widthways, so that the egg yolk is on the outside of the olive. Serve the olives with the sauce spooned over them and the onion and mushroom arranged around them.

RÔTI DE VEAU AUX PETITS OIGNONS (ROAST VEAL WITH BABY ONIONS)

(4 servings)

Preparation time: 30 minutes
Cooking time: 55 minutes

2 medium carrots, thinly sliced
1 large onion, thinly sliced
1 garlic clove, thinly sliced
2 shallots, thinly sliced
3 drops of oil
1kg (2¼lb) veal joint, for roasting
Salt and black pepper
20 baby onions, peeled
2 cloves

Preheat the oven to 220°C/425°F/Gas 7.

Arrange the carrot, onion, garlic and shallot in the bottom of a baking dish (oiled and wiped with kitchen paper). Place the veal on this bed of vegetables. Season with salt and pepper and add a cup of water to the bottom of the dish. Brown the veal for 20 minutes, then take out of the oven and place it in a heated dish. Strain the cooking juices. Put the veal and juices back into the baking dish. Stick the cloves into two of the baby onions and put everything in the dish. Turn the heat down and bake at 190°C/375°F/Gas 5 for about 30 minutes. Serve from the baking dish.

SAUTÉ DE VEAU AU PAPRIKA
(SAUTÉED PAPRIKA VEAL)

(4 servings)

Preparation time: 30 minutes
Cooking time: 1 hour

You will need a steamer.

800g (1¾lb) veal topside, cut into cubes
3 drops of oil
1 large onion, very finely chopped
2 teaspoons paprika
Salt and black pepper
2 tomatoes
2 carrots, cut into thin strips
1 good-sized courgette, cut into long ribbons
200g (7oz) virtually fat-free fromage frais

Season the veal, then brown the pieces in a frying pan (oiled then wiped with kitchen paper) over a medium heat. Continue cooking for 10 minutes, stirring with a spatula. As soon as the meat starts to brown, add the onion and paprika. Season with salt and pepper and stir thoroughly. Turn the heat down low and continue to cook for a further 30 minutes. Halve the tomatoes, remove the seeds, as well as any juice, and cut the tomato flesh into small cubes. Steam the carrot, courgette and tomato for 15 minutes. Just before serving, add the fromage frais. Adjust the seasoning. Transfer the paprika veal to a serving dish and arrange the vegetables around it.

CÔTES DE VEAU VICTORIENNES (VICTORIAN VEAL CHOPS)

(2 servings)

Preparation time: 15 minutes
Cooking time: 50 minutes

500g (1lb 2oz) tinned tomatoes
150g (5½oz) carrots, grated
150g (5½oz) celery, chopped
1 teaspoon finely chopped basil
Salt and black pepper
2 veal chops

Preheat the oven to 180°C/350°F/Gas 4.
Pour the tin of tomatoes into a bowl. Add the carrot, celery, basil, some salt and black pepper. Mix together thoroughly. Place the meat between two layers of this mixture in a small ovenproof dish. Cook for 40–50 minutes.

RÔTI DE VEAU EN SAUCE
(VEAL IN A HERBY TOMATO SAUCE)

(4 servings)

Preparation time: 10 minutes
Cooking time: 1 hour

1kg (2lb 4oz) veal joint, for roasting
Salt and black pepper
1 low-salt veal stock cube
1 garlic clove, finely chopped
1 large shallot, finely chopped
1 tablespoon oregano, herbes de Provence (mixed herbs) and basil
1 tomato, cut into pieces

Season the veal with salt and pepper and brown it in a casserole dish over a high, and then a medium heat. Once the veal has turned a nice colour and is cooked through, remove to a board to rest and add the veal stock cube, diluted in a large cup of water, to the cooking juices in the dish. Now add salt, pepper, the garlic, shallot and herbs to the sauce. When the sauce has reduced a little, add the tomato. Serve the veal presented on a serving dish, accompanied by the sauce, which should be of an even consistency.

FOIE À LA TOMATE
(CALF'S LIVER WITH TOMATO)

(1 serving)

Preparation time: 20 minutes
Cooking time: 20 minutes

100g/3½oz slice of calf's liver
3 drops of oil
1 medium onion, thinly sliced
1 large tomato or 1 tin of chopped tomatoes
½ teaspoon oregano
1 level teaspoon cornflour
Salt and black pepper
Flat-leaf parsley, chopped

Cut up the calf's liver slice diagonally to produce three or four very thin, small escalopes. Preheat a non-stick frying pan (oiled and wiped with kitchen paper) and gently fry the onion. Remove it from the frying pan as soon as it turns golden brown and put to one side. In the same frying pan, fry the tomato, sprinkling it with the oregano. Remove from the heat. Coat the calf's liver slices with cornflour and season with salt and pepper. Fry the liver escalopes on both sides over a medium heat. Place the slices of liver onto a hot plate and arrange the cooked tomato and browned onion around them. Scatter the parsley on top and serve immediately.

TARTE FLAMBÉE ALSACIENNE (ALSATIAN FLAMBÉ TART)

(4 servings)

Preparation time: 15 minutes
Cooking time: 30 minutes

35g (1¼oz) cornflour
2 eggs, separated
200g (7oz) virtually fat-free fromage frais
250g (9oz) shallots, very finely chopped
Salt and black pepper
200g (7oz) extra-lean ham, chopped
2 tomatoes, thinly sliced
90g (3oz) extra-light cream cheese (optional)

Preheat the oven to 220°C/425°F/Gas 7.
Mix together the cornflour, egg yolks and fromage frais. Add the very stiffly beaten egg whites. Pour this all into a pie dish. Sprinkle the shallots over the top. Season with salt and pepper, then add the ham, tomato and cream cheese. Bake in the oven for 25–30 minutes. Serve either hot or cold.

CHAMPIGNONS FARCIS (SPINACH, HAM AND TURKEY STUFFED MUSHROOMS)

(2 servings)

Preparation time: 25 minutes
Cooking time: 35 minutes

100g (3½oz) spinach
½ teaspoon veal stock
400g (14oz) button mushrooms (big enough to stuff)
Juice of 1 lemon
1 garlic clove, chopped
1 slice of extra-lean ham, chopped
2 slices of cooked turkey, chopped
Parsley, chopped
1 tablespoon oat bran
3–4 tablespoons skimmed milk
Salt and black pepper

Preheat the oven to 180°C/350°F/Gas 4.
Cook the spinach for a few minutes in a little salted, boiling water with the veal stock. Separate the mushroom tops from the stalks and sprinkle lemon juice over the tops. Chop up the thoroughly drained spinach and the mushroom stalks. Mix together well with the garlic, ham, turkey, parsley, bran and milk, and then season. Stuff the mushroom tops with this mixture. Bake in the oven for 20–25 minutes.

LAPIN À L'ESTRAGON
(TARRAGON RABBIT)

(4 servings)

Preparation time: 20 minutes
Cooking time: 55 minutes

500g (1lb 2oz) button mushrooms
3 drops of oil
1 rabbit, cut into pieces
3 teaspoons chopped shallot
2 teaspoons chopped garlic
10 sprigs of tarragon
1 sprig of thyme
1 bay leaf
Raspberry vinegar
Salt and black pepper
2 tablespoons virtually fat-free fromage frais

Cook the whole mushrooms in a casserole dish (oiled and wiped with kitchen paper) with the rabbit until just browned. Add the shallot, garlic, half the tarragon leaves, thyme and bay leaf. Moisten with the vinegar, according to personal taste. Season with salt and pepper and mix together thoroughly. Cover and simmer over a gentle heat for about 40 minutes. Take the rabbit out of the casserole dish and reduce the sauce. Add the fromage frais and the rest of the tarragon.

TERRINE DE LAPIN
(RABBIT TERRINE)

(8 servings)

Preparation time: 1 hour
Cooking time: 2 hours 20 minutes

You will need a steamer.

500g (1lb 2oz) boneless rabbit meat, chopped
4 slices of extra-lean ham (or cooked chicken),
    chopped
1 white onion, chopped
3 shallots, chopped
2 eggs, beaten
2 sprigs of parsley, chopped
Salt and black pepper
Lettuce

Preheat the oven to 180°C/350°F/Gas 4.
Steam the rabbit meat for 20 minutes, then whiz it in a blender with the ham, onion and shallot to produce a stuffing-like mixture. Add the beaten eggs and parsley and season. Put the mixture into a terrine dish, place the dish into a bigger dish and fill this *bain-marie* half full with cold water. Bake for 2 hours. Arrange the terrine on plates, on top of a bed of lettuce, seasoned and dressed to taste.

Eggs and vegetables

OMELETTE AU TOFU (TOFU OMELETTE)
(4 servings)

Preparation time: 15 minutes
Cooking time: 5 minutes

2 eggs
Black pepper
2 tablespoons soy sauce
1 garlic clove, finely chopped
½ onion, chopped
400g (14oz) tofu, cut into small cubes
½ green pepper, chopped
3 drops of oil
1 tablespoon parsley, chopped

In a bowl, beat together the eggs with black pepper, the soy sauce, garlic and onion. Add the tofu and green pepper, then mix everything together. Pour the omelette mixture into a frying pan (oiled and wiped with kitchen paper), cover and cook over a gentle heat. Sprinkle with parsley before serving.

CRÊPES DE COURGETTES
(COURGETTE PANCAKES)

(3 servings)

Preparation time: 15 minutes
Cooking time: 4–5 minutes

6 eggs, separated
6 courgettes, very finely chopped
1 garlic clove, chopped
A few sprigs of parsley, chopped
Salt and black pepper
3 drops of oil

Beat the egg whites until stiff. Mix the courgette together with the egg yolks, garlic, parsley, salt and pepper. Gently fold in the egg whites. Cook in a frying pan (oiled and wiped with kitchen paper) over a medium heat, like large pancakes.

PAIN DE COURGETTES AU JAMBON
(COURGETTE AND HAM LOAF)

(4 servings)

Preparation time: 25 minutes
Cooking time: 20 minutes

500g (1lb 2 oz) courgettes, peeled and thinly sliced
Salt and black pepper

4 eggs
100g (3½oz) extra-lean ham
1 tablespoon virtually fat-free quark
1 tablespoon virtually fat-free fromage frais
1 tablespoon extra-light cream cheese (optional)
1 pinch of nutmeg
1 tablespoon cornflour
4 tablespoons skimmed milk

Place the courgette in a microwave dish, pour in a little water and cook for 5 minutes on the maximum setting. Next, drain the courgettes, season and whiz them in a blender with the eggs, ham, quark, fromage frais, cream cheese, pinch of nutmeg, salt and pepper. Beat everything together with a fork until the mixture is smooth. Mix the cornflour with a little cold water, then add to the hot milk and stir this into the courgette and ham mixture. Line a microwave cake tin with greaseproof paper, pour the loaf mixture into the tin and cover with more greaseproof paper. Cook for about 15 minutes in the microwave. Check that the loaf is cooked and leave to rest for 5 minutes before taking it out of the oven.

FRITATA DE THON AUX COURGETTES (TUNA AND COURGETTE FRITTATA)

(4 servings)

Preparation time: 20 minutes (plus 1 hour cooling time)
Cooking time: 20 minutes

3 thin courgettes, diced
1 white onion, thinly sliced
Salt and black pepper
6 eggs
1 tin of tuna, in brine or spring water
2 tablespoons balsamic vinegar

Steam the courgette and onion or cook them in some stock over a medium heat. Season with salt and pepper and stir from time to time. In the meantime, whisk up the eggs and add the flaked tuna, salt and pepper. Add the courgette and onion. Pour the omelette mixture into a frying pan, stir and cover. Cook for 10 minutes over a gentle heat until the eggs have set. Leave to cool for 1 hour, cut into small slices and season with a little vinegar.

ENDIVES À LA ROYALE
(ROYAL BAKED CHICORY)

(4 servings)

Preparation time: 15 minutes
Cooking time: 15 minutes

1kg (2¼lb) chicory
2 eggs
150ml (5fl oz) skimmed milk
Salt and black pepper
1 pinch of grated nutmeg

Preheat the oven to 190°C/375°F/Gas 5.
Peel the chicory, hollow out the bases and cook for 2 minutes in salted, boiling water. Drain very carefully. In a bowl, beat together the eggs and skimmed milk, season with salt and pepper, then add the nutmeg. Arrange the chicory in a baking dish and pour the beaten egg mixture over them. Bake until the eggs have set.

GRATIN D'ENDIVES
(BAKED CHICORY AND EGGS)

(2 servings)

Preparation time: 20 minutes
Cooking time: 30 minutes

You will need a steamer.

3 eggs
2 onions, finely chopped
3 drops of oil
400g (14oz) chicory
Salt and black pepper
400ml (14fl oz) tomato juice

Preheat the oven to 220°C/425°F/Gas 7.
Cook the eggs for 10 minutes in boiling water until hard-boiled. Brown the onion in a frying pan (oiled and wiped with kitchen paper). Steam the chicory, and then place both in a gratin dish. Finely chop the eggs and sprinkle them over the chicory. Add salt and pepper to the tomato juice, pour over the chicory mixture and bake in the oven for 10 minutes.

FROMAGE BLANC AU CONCOMBRE (CUCUMBER FROMAGE FRAIS)

(2 servings)

Preparation time: 10 minutes
No cooking required

250 g (9oz) virtually fat-free fromage frais
½ cucumber, peeled and cut into 1cm (½ inch) cubes
½ garlic clove, crushed
Juice of ½ lemon
Salt and black pepper
¼ yellow pepper (or green), deseeded and cut into
    very thin strips
1 red pepper, deseeded and cut into very thin strips

In a bowl, mix together the fromage frais, cucumber, garlic and lemon juice. Season with salt and pepper. When ready to serve, decorate with the strips of pepper.

SOUFFLÉ DE CONCOMBRE BASILIC (CUCUMBER AND BASIL SOUFFLÉ)

(2 servings)

Preparation time: 20 minutes
Cooking time: 35 minutes

½ cucumber
4 tablespoons virtually fat-free fromage frais
Salt and black pepper
½ bunch of basil
6 egg whites
4 tomatoes
2 onions, thinly sliced
3 drops of oil

Preheat the oven to 200°C/400°F/Gas 6.

Whiz the cucumber in a blender and mix this purée into the fromage frais. Season with salt and pepper. Chop up eight basil leaves and add them to the mixture. Beat the egg whites until stiff and fold them into the cucumber-fromage frais mixture. Poach the tomatoes in boiling water for 30 seconds, then peel and deseed them. Cut the flesh into small cubes. Sweat the onion for a few minutes in a non-stick frying pan over a medium heat without any oil. Add the tomato, season and cook over a gentle heat for 15 minutes. Put a spoonful of the chopped tomato and onion mixture into the bottom of two ramekin dishes (oiled and wiped with kitchen paper), then fill them two-thirds full with the soufflé mixture. Bake for 15 minutes. Once the soufflés are cooked, place a basil leaf on top of each one.

TOMATES AU NID
(STUFFED, BAKED TOMATOES)

(4 servings)

Preparation time: 15 minutes
Cooking time: 30 minutes

8 tomatoes
Salt and black pepper
4 eggs
200g (7oz) extra-lean ham, finely chopped
Fresh basil, very finely chopped

Preheat the oven to 220°C/425°F/Gas 7.
Cut the tops off the tomatoes, spoon out the insides, sprinkle some salt inside and turn them over to degorge their juices. Beat the eggs, season them with salt and pepper, add the ham and a little basil. Divide this mixture among the tomatoes, place them in a baking dish and bake for 25–30 minutes.

OEUFS LORRAINS
(BAKED EGGS WITH A BASIL TOMATO SAUCE)

(2 servings)

Preparation time: 10 minutes
Cooking time: 40 minutes

4 eggs
500ml (18fl oz) skimmed milk
Salt and black pepper
1 pinch of nutmeg
6 tomatoes
A few basil leaves

Preheat the oven to 180°C/350°F/Gas 4.
Beat the eggs with the milk, then add the salt, pepper and nutmeg. Pour into two individual ramekin dishes. Place the dishes into a bigger dish and fill this *bain-marie* half full with cold water. Bake for 40 minutes. In the meantime, prepare a basil-flavoured tomato sauce by heating the tomatoes with the basil. Season with salt and pepper. Turn the baked eggs out of the ramekins and serve hot, surrounded with tomato sauce.

PAPETON D'AUBERGINES
(EGG-BAKED AUBERGINES)

(2 servings)

Preparation time: 20 minutes (plus 30 minutes salting)
Cooking time: 30 minutes

400g (14oz) aubergines, peeled and cut into thick
    slices
Salt and black pepper
3 eggs
200ml (7fl oz) skimmed milk
Nutmeg
A few sprigs of thyme, chopped
A few sprigs of rosemary, chopped

Preheat the oven to 150°C/300°F/Gas 2.
Place the aubergine in a colander, sprinkle with salt
and leave them to degorge their juices for 30 minutes.
Wipe the slices dry, blanch them for 5 minutes in boiling
water and drain. Beat the eggs together and season.
Whisk them into the milk, grate in a little nutmeg
and sprinkle with thyme and rosemary. Arrange the
aubergine slices in a baking dish, pour the egg-milk
mixture over them and bake for 30 minutes.

RUBANS D'OMELETTE AUX ANCHOIS (ANCHOVY OMELETTE STRIPS)

(2 servings)

Preparation time: 15 minutes
Cooking time: 10 minutes

3 tomatoes, quartered
8 tinned anchovies, rinsed and dried
1 tablespoon capers
8 eggs
2 tablespoons skimmed milk
10 chives, finely chopped
5 sprigs of coriander, finely chopped
5 sprigs of parsley, finely chopped
Black pepper
6 sun-dried tomatoes

Fry the tomatoes in a frying pan with the anchovies and capers for 5 minutes over a medium heat. Beat together the eggs, add the milk and herbs and season with pepper. Make two large, thin omelettes with the eggs (about 5mm/¼ inch thick). Leave to cool and cut into strips about 2cm (¾ inch) wide. Place the omelette strips in a dish along with the tomato and anchovies. Add the sun-dried tomatoes and mix everything together well.

SOUFFLÉ AUX MUSHROOMS
(MUSHROOM SOUFFLÉ)

(1 serving)

Preparation time: 15 minutes
Cooking time: 12 minutes

150g (5½oz) button mushrooms
1 egg, separated
3 tablespoons virtually fat-free fromage frais
1 egg white
Salt and black pepper

Preheat the oven to 180°C/350°F/Gas 4.
Drop the mushrooms into a saucepan filled with boiling water and cook for 2 minutes. Whiz them in a blender, then mix this mushroom purée together with the egg yolk, fromage frais and the two stiffly beaten egg whites. Season with salt and pepper and pour into a small ramekin dish. Bake in the oven for about 10 minutes.

TARTE AUX CHAMPIGNONS
(MUSHROOM TART)

(2 servings)

Preparation time: 15 minutes
Cooking time: 40 minutes

3 eggs
700ml (1¼ pints) skimmed milk
2 teaspoons yeast
Salt and black pepper
1 small pepper, chopped into very small pieces
1 courgette, chopped into very small pieces
4 large button mushrooms, chopped into very small
 pieces
1 small onion, chopped into very small pieces

Preheat the oven to 230°C/450°F/Gas 8.
Whisk together the eggs, milk and yeast in a bowl and
season with salt and pepper. Add all the vegetables to
the egg mixture. Pour into a non-stick tin and bake for
about 40 minutes.

FLAN AUX LÉGUMES
(VEGETABLE TART)

(2 servings)

Preparation time: 10 minutes
Cooking time: 15 minutes

4 eggs
1 pinch of nutmeg
1 tablespoon chopped herbs
500ml (18fl oz) skimmed milk
200g (7oz) vegetables (tomatoes, courgettes,
    broccoli, aubergines, carrots), chopped
Salt and black pepper

Preheat the oven to 180°C/350°F/Gas 4.
Beat the eggs, nutmeg and herbs together in a baking
dish, then pour over the milk, which has been heated
slightly. Add the vegetables and place the dish into a
bigger dish and fill this *bain-marie* half full with cold
water. Bake for 15 minutes.

FLAN DE LÉGUMES À LA PROVENÇALE (PROVENÇAL VEGETABLE TART)

(4 servings)

Preparation time: 35 minutes
Cooking time: 55 minutes

4 tomatoes
500g (1lb 2oz) courgettes, cut into small pieces
    without removing the skin
2 red peppers, deseeded and finely chopped
1 onion, thinly sliced
3 drops of oil
Salt and black pepper
4 eggs
4 tablespoons skimmed milk
1 tablespoon extra-light cream cheese (optional)

Preheat the oven to 200°C/400°F/Gas 6.
Poach the tomatoes in boiling water for 30 seconds, then peel, deseed and dice them. Fry all the vegetables in a frying pan (oiled and wiped with kitchen paper) over a high heat for 20 minutes. Season with salt and pepper. Beat together the eggs, add the milk and cream cheese, and then season with salt and pepper. Add in all the vegetables, mix together well and pour into a non-stick cake tin. Place the tin into a bigger dish and fill this *bain-marie* half full with cold water. Bake for 30 minutes.

Seafood, fish and vegetables

CALAMARS À LA PROVENÇALE
(PROVENÇAL CALAMARI)
(4 servings)

Preparation time: 20 minutes
Cooking time: 1 hour 5 minutes

1–2 onions, finely chopped
3 drops of oil
2 tins of chopped tomatoes
2–3 garlic cloves, very finely chopped
1 pepper, diced
1 bouquet garni
1 chilli pepper, very finely chopped
Salt and black pepper
500g (1lb 2oz) calamari rings, cleaned

Over a gentle heat, fry the onion in a frying pan (oiled and wiped with kitchen paper). When the onion is nicely browned, add the chopped tomatoes, garlic, pepper, bouquet garni, chilli pepper, salt and pepper.

Cook for 10 minutes over a gentle heat with the lid on. Add the calamari to the sauce and cook over a gentle heat, with the lid on, for 45 minutes.

RAGOÛT DE MOULES AUX POIREAUX (MUSSEL STEW WITH LEEKS)

(4 servings)

Preparation time: 30 minutes
Cooking time: 30 minutes

2 litres (3½ pints) mussels, scrubbed and rinsed well
1kg (2¼lb) leeks
Salt and black pepper
1 pinch of grated nutmeg
150ml (5fl oz) *Sauce Blanche* (see page 366)
1 bunch of parsley, very finely chopped
1 bunch of chervil, very finely chopped
1 sprig of tarragon, very finely chopped
Juice of ½ very ripe lemon

Get the mussels to open up in a casserole dish over a high heat, stirring frequently. Remove them from their shells (discard any that have not opened) and keep the cooking water. Strain it and then pour it into a high-sided frying pan. Peel the leeks, removing some of the green part. Wash and slice them up, cover and poach for 5 minutes in the mussel water, then remove the lid and cook for 20 minutes with the salt, pepper and grated nutmeg. Prepare the white sauce. Stir the herbs into the white sauce and add the shelled mussels. Sprinkle over the lemon juice. Once the leeks are cooked, add the white sauce, mixing it in carefully. Serve piping hot.

GRATIN DE MOULES CRÈME FRAICHE (BAKED MUSSELS)

(4 servings)

Preparation time: 30 minutes
Cooking time: 25 minutes

3 drops of oil
750g (1lb 10oz) courgettes, sliced
Salt and black pepper
1kg (2¼lb) mussels, scrubbed and rinsed well
1 bay leaf
2 teaspoons cornflour
2 teaspoons crème fraîche (less than 5% fat) (optional)
8 egg yolks
8 teaspoons virtually fat-free fromage frais
6 tablespoons extra-light cream cheese (optional)

Preheat the oven to 240°C/475°F/Gas 9.
In a frying pan (oiled and wiped with kitchen paper), cook the courgette over a medium heat. Season with salt and pepper, stir and leave them to give off

water for 10 minutes, then drain. In the meantime, cook the mussels in a large saucepan with the bay leaf, drain them (discarding any that haven't opened) and keep the cooking juices. Remove the shells and strain the juices. In a saucepan but off the heat, blend the cornflour with a cup of the cooled juice from the mussels and the crème fraîche. Add pepper, heat and whisk and allow to thicken, then remove from the heat. In a bowl, mix together the egg yolks and fromage frais. Add the sauce to this mixture, stirring continuously. Put the courgettes in a gratin dish, spread the mussels out on top of them, pour over the sauce and dot with the cream cheese. Place in the oven for 5 minutes, then under the grill for 2 minutes.

AMUSE-GUEULES RÉGIME
(SEAFOOD AND CRUDITÉS WITH A HERB CREAM)
(6 servings)

Preparation time: 30 minutes
No cooking required

1 cucumber
3 carrots
1 bunch of radishes
1 fennel bulb
A few sticks of celery
200g (7oz) cooked prawns
200g (7oz) seafood sticks (surimi)

For the herb cream
250g (9oz) virtually fat-free fromage frais
A few basil leaves
A few sprigs of tarragon
A few sprigs of parsley
Salt and black pepper

Peel all the washed vegetables and cut them into crudité sticks. Shell the prawns. Mix together all the ingredients for the herb cream and serve with the crudités, prawns and seafood sticks.

CREVETTES À LA TOMATE
(TOMATOES STUFFED WITH PRAWNS)
(2 servings)

Preparation time: 15 minutes
Cooking time: 10 minutes

500g (1lb 2oz) tomatoes
600g (1¼lb) Mediterranean prawns, cooked and
   shelled
4 eggs

For the sauce
2 hard-boiled egg yolks
1 teaspoon mustard
1 tablespoon lemon juice

150g (5½oz) fat-free natural yoghurt
Salt and black pepper

Cook the eggs for 10 minutes in boiling water until hard-boiled. Delicately scoop out the insides of the tomatoes, sprinkle the shells with salt and turn them over. Blend the shelled prawns with two of the hard-boiled eggs and stuff the tomatoes with this mixture. To make the sauce, crush the yolks of the two remaining hard-boiled eggs with the teaspoon of mustard. Pour in the lemon juice and season with salt and pepper, then gradually work in the yoghurt, stirring all the time. Cover the stuffed tomatoes with this sauce.

POÊLÉE DE SURIMI ET CREVETTES AUX CHAMPIGNONS (STIR-FRIED GARLIC PRAWNS AND MUSHROOMS)

(4 servings)

Preparation time: 25 minutes
Cooking time: 7–8 minutes

500g (1lb 2oz) large prawns, shelled and chopped
2 garlic cloves, chopped
500g (1lb 2oz) button mushrooms, thinly sliced
500g (1lb 2oz) seafood sticks (surimi), cut into cubes
Salt and black pepper
1 bunch of parsley, chopped

In a non-stick frying pan, fry the prawns and garlic over a medium heat, then add the mushrooms. Braise for 1 minute, then add the seafood sticks. Season, stir in the parsley and serve immediately.

ROULADES DE CONCOMBRE AUX CREVETTES (CUCUMBER ROULADES WITH PRAWNS)

(2 servings)

Preparation time: 20 minutes
No cooking required

2 eggs
100g (3½oz) prawns, cooked and shelled
100g (3½oz) virtually fat-free fromage frais
A few drops of Tabasco
Salt and black pepper
½ cucumber
4 tablespoons chopped chives

Cook the eggs for 10 minutes in boiling water until hard-boiled. Crush with a fork and mix together with the prawns, fromage frais and Tabasco. Season with salt and pepper and put to one side. Peel the cucumber, scoop out the middle and cut it into slices lengthways. Pour the prawn sauce over the cucumber and sprinkle the chives on top. Roll the cucumber slices onto each other, arrange on plates and serve very cold.

SALADE DE CREVETTES
(PRAWN AND EGG SALAD)

(2 servings)

Preparation time: 15 minutes
Cooking time: 5 minutes

1 teaspoon olive oil
4 teaspoons cider vinegar
Salt and black pepper
600g (1¼lb) lettuce
A few sprigs of tarragon
200g (7oz) prawns, cooked and shelled
4 eggs

Make up the vinaigrette in a bowl with the olive oil, vinegar and some seasoning. Mix together the lettuce, tarragon leaves and shelled prawns in another bowl. Soft-boil the eggs for 5–6 minutes in boiling water. Shell them carefully as the yolks will still be runny. Place them, whilst still very hot, on top of the dressed lettuce and prawns.

POISSON AU GRATIN
(PRAWN AND ASPARAGUS BAKED FISH)

(2 servings)

Preparation time: 15 minutes
Cooking time: 30 minutes

500g (1lb 2oz) white fish fillets (cod, sea bream,
    pollock or coley)
4 tablespoons virtually fat-free fromage frais
4 egg whites
125g (4½oz) shelled prawns
1 tin of asparagus spears
A few sprigs of parsley
Salt and black pepper

Preheat the oven to 180°C/350°F/Gas 4.
Mix together the fish fillets, fromage frais and egg
whites. Put this mixture into a dish along with the
prawns, asparagus and parsley. Bake in the oven for
30 minutes.

SCAMPIS À LA MEXICAINE
(MEXICAN GREEN CHILLI DUBLIN BAY PRAWNS)

(3–4 servings)

Preparation time: 10 minutes
Cooking time: 3 minutes

You will need a steamer.

4 tomatoes
1 green chilli, deseeded and chopped
2 tablespoons coriander, chopped
Juice of 1 lime
1 garlic clove, crushed
Salt
32 Dublin Bay prawns

Poach the tomatoes in boiling water for 30 seconds, then peel and deseed them. Dice the tomatoes, then mix them together with the green chilli. Add the coriander, lime juice, garlic and salt. Steam the Dublin Bay prawns for 2–3 minutes and mix them into the sauce.

PAIN AU SURIMI
(SEAFOOD BREAD)

(2 servings)

Preparation time: 10 minutes
Cooking time: 30 minutes

300g (10½oz) seafood sticks (surimi)
8 eggs
1 tin of tomato purée
3 tablespoons virtually fat-free fromage frais
A few sprigs of parsley
Salt and black pepper

Preheat the oven to 160°C/325°F/Gas 3.
Mix all the ingredients together thoroughly. Pour into a tin and cook for 30 minutes. Eat once cold.

ASPERGES AU SURIMI
(ASPARAGUS WITH SEAFOOD STICKS)

(2 servings)

Preparation time: 10 minutes
Cooking time: 20 minutes

4 eggs
500g (1lb 2oz) asparagus
1 vegetable stock cube
2 tomatoes
10 seafood sticks (surimi)
1 lettuce
Vinaigrette Maya (see page 357)

Cook the eggs for 10 minutes in boiling water until hard-boiled. Peel the asparagus and snap off the woody bottoms of the asparagus spears at their natural breaking point. Cook in salted boiling water, flavoured with the stock cube, for 5–10 minutes, until the asparagus stalks are tender. Once the asparagus is cooked, drain it. Chop the asparagus, tomatoes and seafood sticks into pieces and add to a bowl. Halve the eggs lengthways and add. Clean the lettuce and keep the best leaves. Arrange them in a star shape in the bottom of a round dish, placing an equal amount of the asparagus, tomato, hard-boiled eggs and seafood stick mixture on each leaf. Serve with the *Vinaigrette Maya*.

COQUILLES SAINT-JACQUES
(COQUILLES SAINT-JACQUES)

(2 servings)

Preparation time: 15 minutes
Cooking time: 20 minutes

6–8 scallops
Salt and black pepper
200g (7oz) sorrel
2 nice shallots, finely chopped
3 drops of oil
4 teaspoons virtually fat-free fromage frais

In a frying pan, quickly brown the seasoned scallops over a high heat, then remove and keep to one side. Place the sorrel in the frying pan and cook over a medium heat for 10 minutes. Meanwhile, heat the shallot in another frying pan (oiled and wiped with kitchen paper) and when soft, add the fromage frais. Place a spoonful of sorrel onto the plates, add the scallops on top of the sorrel and pour the warm sauce over them.

GRATIN DE PÉTONCLES AUX ÉPINARDS (SCALLOP AND SPINACH BAKE)

(2 servings)

Preparation time: 30 minutes
Cooking time: 15 minutes

475g (1lb 1oz) small scallops
500g (1lb 2oz) fresh spinach
2 egg yolks
3 tablespoons virtually fat-free fromage frais
15g (½oz) cornflour
300ml (10fl oz) fish stock
Salt and black pepper

Preheat the oven to 200°C/400°F/Gas 6.
Sauté the scallops in a frying pan over a medium heat. Put to one side. Wash, dry and very finely chop the spinach. Add the scallops. Fry for a few minutes over a gentle heat, then keep warm. Mix together the egg yolks and fromage frais in a saucepan. Blend the cornflour with the cold fish stock, add to the pan and season with salt and pepper. Divide the scallop and spinach mixture between two individual gratin dishes, pour the sauce over and brown for 15 minutes. Serve in the gratin dishes.

MARINADE DE SAINT-JACQUES AUX LÉGUMES GRILLÉS (SCALLOP AND GRILLED VEGETABLES SALAD)

(2 servings)

Preparation time: 10 minutes (plus 1 hour marinating)
Cooking time: 25 minutes

You will need a steamer.

Zest and juice of 1 lemon
2 tablespoons coriander, finely chopped
Salt and black pepper
16 scallops
1 aubergine, cut into cubes
2 courgettes, sliced
4 tablespoons tomato sauce, such as *Sauce de Paprika aux Poivrons* (see page 369) or *Sauce Grelette* (see page 370)

Prepare a marinade by mixing together the lemon zest and juice, coriander, salt and pepper. Steam the scallops for 3 minutes. Steam the vegetables for 10 minutes, then cook them for 10 minutes in a frying pan covered with a sheet of greaseproof paper. Pour the marinade over the grilled vegetables. Spread the tomato sauce onto two plates, then add the vegetables and next the scallops and leave to marinate for 1 hour in the fridge before serving.

MOUSSE DE BROCOLIS AU SURIMI (BROCCOLI AND SEAFOOD MOUSSE)

(6 servings)

Preparation time: 15 minutes (plus 4 hours chilling time)
Cooking time: 10 minutes

6 gelatine leaves
1kg (2¼lb) frozen broccoli purée
12 teaspoons virtually fat-free fromage frais
280g (10oz) seafood sticks (surimi), grated
Salt and black pepper
1 jar of tomato purée
1 teaspoon frozen basil
½ teaspoon frozen garlic

Soak the gelatine leaves in a bowl of cold water for a few minutes. Cook the broccoli purée in the microwave for about 10 minutes. Next, work the gelatine into the hot broccoli, followed by the fromage frais, diluted with a tiny bit of water to bind the purée, and the seafood sticks. Season with salt and pepper. Divide the mousse among six individual ramekin dishes, lined with clingfilm so that the mousses are easier to turn out. Leave to set in the fridge for at least 4 hours. Prepare the tomato coulis by mixing together the tomato purée with the basil, garlic, salt and pepper. Keep cool. To serve, turn the mousses out onto plates and divide the tomato coulis among them. Serve immediately.

CRÈME DE THON (TUNA CREAM)

(2 servings)

Preparation time: 10 minutes
Cooking time: 25 minutes

200g (7oz) tuna, in brine or spring water, flaked
1 onion, finely chopped
1 garlic clove, finely chopped
300g (10½oz) courgettes, peeled and thinly sliced
3 tablespoons tomato purée
Black pepper

Heat 500ml (18fl oz) water in a saucepan. Put the tuna, onion, garlic, courgette and tomato purée into the salted water and add black pepper. Cover and cook for 25 minutes.

QUICHE SANS PÂTE THON ET TOMATES (TUNA AND TOMATO PASTRY-FREE QUICHE)

(3 servings)

Preparation time: 15 minutes
Cooking time: 25 minutes

2 whole eggs
4 egg whites
3 drops of oil
2 small tomatoes, very thinly sliced

1 small tin of tuna, in brine or spring water, flaked
2 tablespoons virtually fat-free fromage frais
2 pinches of herbes de Provence (mixed herbs)
Salt and black pepper

Preheat the oven to 180°C/350°F/Gas 4.
Beat together the eggs and the egg whites, then make an omelette in a frying pan (oiled and wiped with kitchen paper). Put into a baking dish, then mix together all the remaining ingredients and add to the dish. Bake for 20–25 minutes.

TOMATES AU THON ET AUX CAPERS (TUNA AND CAPER-FILLED TOMATOES)

(3 servings)

Preparation time: 20 minutes
No cooking required

8 tomatoes
Salt and black pepper
1 tin of tuna, in brine or spring water
100g (3½oz) virtually fat-free fromage frais
2 tablespoons capers, drained
2 tablespoons chives, very finely chopped
1 tablespoon lemon juice
2 tablespoons trout roe
4 pinches of paprika

For a more sophisticated dish, poach the tomatoes in boiling water for 30 seconds before peeling away the skin. Slice off the tops of the tomatoes and leave to one side. Scoop out the insides, sprinkle some salt inside and turn them upside down onto some kitchen paper. Mix together the flaked tuna, fromage frais, capers, chives and lemon juice. Add some pepper and then stuff the tomatoes with this mixture. Garnish the stuffed tomatoes with the trout roe and paprika. Finally, put their tops back on.

PIZZA AU THON
(TUNA PIZZA)

(1 serving)

Preparation time: 20 minutes
Cooking time: 1 hour 15 minutes

For the base (using the galette recipe)
2 tablespoons oat bran
1 tablespoon virtually fat-free fat fromage frais
50g (1¾oz) virtually fat-free quark
3 eggs, separated
Salt and black pepper

For the topping
1 large onion, finely chopped
3 drops of oil

500g (1lb 2oz) chopped tomatoes, drained
1 teaspoon thyme, oregano and basil
2 pinches of black pepper
Salt
175g (6oz) tuna, in brine or spring water, drained and
   chopped
2 tablespoons capers
6 teaspoons low-fat cream cheese (optional)

Preheat the oven to 190°C/375°F/Gas 5.

Mix together all the ingredients for the base (this is the same as the galette recipe), except the egg whites, until the mixture is smooth. Finally, work in the stiffly beaten egg whites. Once the mixture is ready, pour it into a warmed frying pan and cook over a medium heat for about 30 minutes, using a spatula to turn it over, and then continue cooking for a further 5 minutes on the other side. Meanwhile, gently fry the onion in a non-stick frying pan (oiled and wiped with kitchen paper), add the tomatoes, herbs, pepper and salt. Simmer over a gentle heat for 10 minutes. Spread the tomato mixture over the base, scatter over the tuna, capers and cream cheese. Bake in the oven for 25 minutes.

THON AUX TROIS POIVRONS (THREE PEPPER TUNA)

(2 servings)

Preparation time: 20 minutes (plus 2–3 hours marinating)
Cooking time: 40 minutes

You will need a steamer.

1 red pepper
1 green pepper
1 yellow pepper
3 drops of oil
1 tuna steak, weighing 700g (1lb 9oz)
Salt and white pepper
Juice of 1–2 lemons
2 garlic cloves, crushed

Grill the peppers for 10–15 minutes until charred all over. Place in a plastic bag and leave to cool, before peeling away the skin and seeds. Cut the peppers into strips and gently fry for a few minutes over a medium heat in a non-stick frying pan (oiled and wiped with kitchen paper) with a little water in the bottom. Season the tuna and steam for 20 minutes. Mix together the lemon juice, garlic and peppers. Once the tuna is cooked, allow to cool, then marinate it with the peppers in a cool place for 2–3 hours, turning the tuna over regularly. Serve cold.

CONCOMBRE FARCI AU THON
(TUNA-STUFFED CUCUMBER)

(1 serving)

Preparation time: 15 minutes
No cooking required

1 cucumber
125g (4½oz) tin of tuna, in brine or spring water
4 teaspoons *Dukan Mayonnaise* (see page 358)
Salt and black pepper

Peel the cucumber, halve, then cut each one in half again. Deseed with a spoon, leaving at least a 1cm (½inch) edge. In a bowl, mix together the flaked tuna and mayonnaise. Adjust the seasoning. Stuff the cucumber with the tuna mixture.

FILET DE MERLAN À LA NORMANDE
(NORMANDY WHITING FILLETS)

(2 servings)

Preparation time: 20 minutes
Cooking time: 25 minutes

150g (5½oz) mussels, scrubbed and rinsed well
300g (10½oz) whiting fillets
1 bay leaf
A few sprigs of thyme

1 teaspoon chopped garlic
1 teaspoon tomato purée
4 teaspoons virtually fat-free fromage frais
Salt and black pepper

Cook the mussels for 8–10 minutes, covered, in a frying pan, until all the shells have opened. Discard any mussels that haven't opened. Remove the shells and keep back 100ml (3½fl oz) of the liquid. Simmer the fish fillets in a casserole dish with the bay leaf, thyme, garlic and liquid from the mussels for 10 minutes. Remove the fish from the casserole dish and put the tomato purée, fromage frais and mussels in the dish. Cook for 2 minutes over a low heat, season, and then cover the fish with the sauce.

FILET DE SOLE (QUICK FILLET OF SOLE)
(1 serving)

Preparation time: 10 minutes
Cooking time: 2 minutes

You will need a microwave.

200g (7oz) sole fillet
1 fresh tomato, finely chopped
1 garlic clove, chopped
A few capers
4 basil leaves

Place the fillet of sole in a microwave-safe dish. Mix together the tomato, garlic, capers and basil in another dish. Spread this mixture over the fillet of fish and cover. Cook in the microwave for 2 minutes on high.

RAMEQUINS DE POISSON AU COULIS DE TOMATES (SOLE RAMEKINS WITH TOMATO SAUCE)

(2 servings)

Preparation time: 25 minutes
Cooking time: 45 minutes

800g (1lb 12oz) tomatoes
400g (14oz) sole fillets
Salt and black pepper
1 bunch of chervil
1 egg
2 generous tablespoons virtually fat-free fromage frais
3 drops of oil
1 sprig of thyme
1 small bay leaf branch
1 garlic clove, crushed
1 shallot, chopped

Preheat the oven to 200°C/400°F/Gas 6.
Poach the tomatoes in boiling water for 30 seconds, then peel them. Flake or blend the sole fillets, season with salt and pepper, and add the leaves from the

bunch of chervil, the beaten egg and fromage frais. Pour into two ramekin dishes (oiled and wiped with kitchen paper) and cook for 20–25 minutes. Wait a few minutes before turning the fish ramekins out. In the meantime, prepare the sauce from the peeled tomatoes blended and cooked for a good 15 minutes with the thyme, bay leaf, garlic clove and shallot. When ready to serve, pour this sauce over the fish.

SOLE CRUE SUR CONCASSÉE DE TOMATES (SOLE CEVICHE ON CHOPPED TOMATOES)

(2 servings)

Preparation time: 10 minutes (plus 1 hour
    refrigeration)
No cooking required

4 ripe tomatoes
1 lemon
Salt and black pepper
4 sole fillets, cut into very thin strips
1 small sprig of mint, very finely chopped
1 sprig of chervil, very finely chopped
1 sprig of parsley, very finely chopped

Poach the tomatoes in boiling water for 30 seconds, then peel and deseed them. Finely chop and season with the lemon, salt and pepper. Divide the tomato between the plates. Coat the thin strips of sole with the herbs and place them on top of the tomatoes. Refrigerate for 1 hour.

FILET DE SOLE À L'OSEILLE
(FILLET OF SOLE WITH SORREL)

(2 servings)

Preparation time: 20 minutes (plus 2 hours marinating)
Cooking time: 4 minutes

4 sole fillets
Juice of 2 lemons
10 small sorrel leaves, chopped
Salt and black pepper

Marinate the sole fillets for at least 2 hours in the lemon juice and chopped sorrel, then drain. Grill the marinated fillets on both sides in a non-stick frying pan. Season with salt and pepper. Serve the fillets with the marinade juices drizzled over them.

AILE DE RAIE AU SAFRAN
(SAFFRON SKATE WING)

(2 servings)

Preparation time: 20 minutes
Cooking time: 45 minutes

2 leeks (white part only), chopped
2 carrots, chopped
2 sticks of celery, chopped
1 onion, studded with 1 clove
1 bouquet garni
5 black peppercorns
1 tiny pinch of saffron
Salt
1 nice skate wing, weighing about 400g (14 oz)
1 tablespoon chopped parsley

Cook the leek, carrot and celery in 1 litre (1¾ pints) salted boiling water for 10 minutes. Add the onion, bouquet garni, peppercorns and saffron. Cover and continue cooking over a gentle heat for 25 minutes, then remove the vegetables using a draining spoon and check the seasoning. Drop the skate wing into the simmering stock and poach it for 10 minutes. Drain and serve surrounded by the vegetables, with a ladleful of the stock poured over the dish and sprinkled with parsley.

SALADE TIÈDE DE HARICOTS ET AILE DE RAIE (WARM SKATE AND GREEN BEAN SALAD)

(2 servings)

Preparation time: 25 minutes
Cooking time: 15 minutes

2 litres (3½ pints) court bouillon or fish stock
2 skate wings
100g (3½oz) French beans
1 tablespoon raspberry vinegar
A few drops of hazelnut or other vegetable oil
Salt and black pepper
1 garlic clove
1 shallot

Prepare the court bouillon or stock, bring to the boil and poach the skate wing in it, leaving it to simmer for 8 minutes. In the meantime, steam or boil the French beans. Make up some vinaigrette with the raspberry vinegar and oil (heighten the taste slightly with a little hazelnut oil). Crush together some pepper with the garlic and shallot and stir into the vinaigrette, seasoning with salt. Place the French beans in a bowl with two-thirds of the vinaigrette. Mix together, then arrange on plates and place the skate on top (having previously removed any skin or cartilage). Pour over the rest of the vinaigrette and serve straightaway.

AILE DE RAIE À LA CRÉOLE
(CREOLE SKATE WING)

(2 servings)

Preparation time: 25 minutes (plus 2 hours
  refrigeration)
Cooking time: 20 minutes

300g (10½oz) skate wing
25g (1oz) gelatine
150g (5½oz) lettuce
1 lime, quartered
5–6 mint leaves

For the court bouillon
1 garlic clove
1 onion, studded with a clove
A few sprigs of thyme
1 carrot
Salt and black pepper

Place the skate in a saucepan of water flavoured with
the court bouillon ingredients. Cover and cook for 20
minutes over a medium heat. Drain the skate, reserving
the cooking liquid, and leave to cool. Remove the skin
and fillet the fish, then chop it up. Strain the court
bouillon through a very fine sieve. Dissolve the gelatine
in 500ml (18fl oz) of this court bouillon and mix in the
chopped fish. Leave to cool. Pour this mixture into two

cake tins and keep refrigerated for 2 hours. To turn the fish out, submerge the moulds carefully into some hot water, then ease the fish out onto a bed of lettuce. Serve this dish cold, decorated with the lime quarters and mint leaves.

CABILLAUD AU SAFRAN (SAFFRON COD)

(4 servings)

Preparation time: 15 minutes
Cooking time: 40 minutes

500g (1lb 2oz) tomatoes, cut into chunks
2 garlic cloves, crushed
100g (3½oz) leek (white part only), finely chopped
100g (3½oz) onions, chopped
1 fennel bulb, finely chopped
3 sprigs of parsley
1 pinch of saffron
Salt and black pepper
4 slices of cod

Add the tomato, garlic, leek, onion, fennel, parsley and saffron to a casserole dish. Season with salt and pepper and simmer for 30 minutes. Add the fish and cover with 100ml (3½fl oz) water. Turn up the heat, then reduce the heat and simmer for 10 minutes.

CABILLAUD COCOTTE
(COD AND THYME COURGETTES)

(2 servings)

Preparation time: 10 minutes
Cooking time: 20 minutes

300g (10½oz) courgettes, peeled and sliced
300g (10½oz) cod fillet, sliced
Salt and black pepper
1 garlic clove, crushed
Thyme

In a non-stick casserole dish, arrange a layer of courgettes, then a layer of fish and season with salt and pepper. Finish off with a layer of courgettes. Add salt and pepper again, as well as the garlic and thyme. Cover and cook over a very gentle heat for 20 minutes.

RÔTI DE CABILLAUD AUX COURGETTES ET À LA TOMATE (ROAST COD WITH COURGETTES AND TOMATO)

(4 servings)

Preparation time: 20 minutes
Cooking time: 30 minutes

300g (10½oz) tomatoes
400g (14oz) courgettes, cut into 3mm (¹/₈ inch) thick slices
2 sprigs of thyme
Salt and black pepper
1 cod steak, weighing 700g (1lb 9oz)
4 garlic cloves, cut into 3 slices each

Preheat the oven to 220°C/425°F/Gas 7.
Poach the tomatoes in boiling water for 30 seconds, peel and deseed them, then finely chop the flesh. Pour 1 tablespoon water and the vegetables into a rectangular baking dish. Sprinkle over the crumbled thyme, season with salt and pepper and mix together well. Make six incisions in each side of the fish, insert the garlic slices and season with salt and pepper. Place the fish directly in the centre of the dish, moving the vegetables to the sides, and bake for 30 minutes, stirring the vegetables several times so that they cook evenly. When the fish is cooked, remove the skin, take off the fillets and arrange on serving plates with the vegetables. Pour over the cooking juices and serve immediately.

CABILLAUD AU CURRY
(CURRIED COD)

(4 servings)

Preparation time: 20 minutes
Cooking time: 30 minutes

1 onion, chopped
3 garlic cloves, crushed
4 dried chilli peppers, finely chopped
4 rocotillo chilli peppers (or other mild chilli)
3 drops of oil
1 teaspoon coriander seeds
1 teaspoon ground turmeric
1 teaspoon ground cumin
500g (1lb 2oz) tomatoes, chopped
4 tablespoons water
3 tablespoons lemon juice
700g (1lb 9oz) cod, filleted and cut into pieces
Salt and black pepper

Fry the onion, garlic and chillies gently in a non-stick saucepan (oiled and wiped with kitchen paper). Add the spices and cook for 5 minutes. Mix in the tomatoes, 4 tablespoons water and the lemon juice. Bring everything to the boil. Reduce the heat and leave to simmer for 15 minutes with the lid on. Next add the cubes of fish. Season with salt and pepper and continue cooking for 10 minutes over a gentle heat.

CABILLAUD AUX HERBES
(COD WITH HERBS AND PEPPERS)

(4 servings)

Preparation time: 20 minutes
Cooking time: 15 minutes

1 shallot, finely chopped
1 onion, finely chopped
1 bunch of herbs, finely chopped
600g (1¼lb) cod fillet
Salt and black pepper
1 red pepper, quartered and deseeded
4 small chilli peppers, halved
Zest and juice of 1 lemon

Preheat the oven to 220°C/425°F/Gas 7.
Mix the shallot and onion with the herbs. Prepare four rectangles of aluminium foil and place a fillet of fish onto each one. Season with salt and pepper. Cover the fish with a pepper quarter, a thin layer of the herb mixture and a chilli pepper. Squeeze the lemon juice over the fish and scatter over the zest. Carefully seal the foil parcels, put them onto a baking sheet and place in the oven. Bake the parcels for 15 minutes.

CASSOLETTES DE CABILLAUD À LA PROVENÇALE (PROVENCE BAKED COD)

(4 servings)

Preparation time: 25 minutes
Cooking time: 15 minutes

8 slices of extra-lean ham
8 tomatoes
Salt and black pepper
2 onions, thinly sliced
2 garlic cloves, thinly sliced
4 cod fillets
A few basil leaves

Preheat the oven to 240°C/475°F/Gas 9.
Place a slice of ham into four small gratin dishes. Poach the tomatoes in boiling water for 30 seconds, then peel and deseed them. Slice and divide the tomatoes out between the gratin dishes. Add salt. Spread the onion and garlic over the tomato. Wrap the remaining slices of ham around the cod fillets and place one in each dish. Season. Bake for 10–15 minutes and, once cooked, add some black pepper and sprinkle the basil leaves on top.

CARRÉ DE BROCOLI ET SAUMON
(SQUARE BAKED SALMON AND BROCCOLI)

(3 servings)

Preparation time: 15 minutes
Cooking time: 35 minutes

2 eggs
2 x 175g (6oz) tins of salmon, in brine or spring water
300g (10½oz) broccoli florets
250g (9oz) virtually fat-free cottage cheese
1 small onion, finely chopped
200g (7oz) green pepper, chopped
Salt and black pepper

Preheat the oven to 180°C/350°F/Gas 4.
Mix together the beaten eggs, drained salmon, broccoli florets, cottage cheese, onion, green pepper, pepper and salt. Place the mixture into a square non-stick dish. Bake for about 35 minutes. Accompany this dish with a salad or vegetables of your choice.

ROULÉS DE SAUMON
(SALMON ROLLS)

(8 servings)

Preparation time: 20 minutes
Cooking time: 20 minutes

2 tins of palm hearts
8 slices of smoked salmon
50g (1¾oz) virtually fat-free quark
125g (4½oz) virtually fat-free fromage frais
2 pinches of herbes de Provence (mixed herbs)
1 drop of raspberry vinegar
Salt and black pepper

Preheat the oven to 150°C/300°F/Gas 2.
Wrap the palm hearts in the smoked salmon slices. Mix together the quark, fromage frais, herbs, vinegar, salt and pepper. Pour half of the fromage frais mixture into a dish, place the salmon rolls on top and cover with the rest of the mixture. Bake in the oven for 20 minutes.

ÉMINCÉ DE SAUMON SUR UN LIT DE POIREAUX (SALMON SLICES ON A BED OF LEEKS)

(2–3 servings)

Preparation time: 15 minutes
Cooking time: 30 minutes

4 tablespoons shallots, chopped
500g (1lb 2oz) leeks, chopped into pieces
Salt and black pepper
4 salmon fillets
1 tablespoon dill

Cook the shallot and leek in a high-sided frying pan over a gentle heat for 20 minutes, adding a little water if necessary. Season with salt and pepper and keep warm. Season the salmon fillets with salt and pepper and place them, skin side down, in a non-stick frying pan. Cook for 10 minutes over a medium heat. Arrange the salmon on the bed of leeks, with the dill sprinkled on top.

FRISÉE AU SAUMON
(CURLY ENDIVE SALMON)

(1 serving)

Preparation time: 10 minutes
No cooking required

60g (2¼oz) smoked salmon, cut into even strips
1 curly endive lettuce heart
A few sprigs of dill
Salt and black pepper
Juice of 1 lemon
1 tablespoon salmon roe

Put the salmon in a salad bowl with the lettuce and dill. Dress with a vinaigrette made from the salt, pepper and lemon juice. Scatter over the salmon roe and serve immediately.

SAUMON GOURMAND
(MOUTHWATERING SALMON APPETIZERS)

(2 servings)

Preparation time: 20 minutes
No cooking required

Juice of ½ lemon
Salt and black pepper
300g (10½oz) fat-free natural yoghurt
½ fennel bulb, cut into small chunks
1 small bunch of dill, finely chopped
4 slices of smoked salmon
4 lettuce leaves

In a small bowl, prepare the sauce by mixing together the lemon juice, salt, pepper and yoghurt. Add the fennel chunks and dill. Just before serving the dish, cut the salmon slices into thin strips and divide between the plates. Serve the sauce in the lettuce leaves.

TIMBALE AUX TROIS SALMONS
(THREE SALMON TIMBALE)

(4 servings)

Preparation time: 20 minutes (plus 2 hours setting time)
Cooking time: 10 minutes

You will need a steamer.

4 small salmon steaks
2 low-salt fish stock cubes
8 gelatine leaves
4 sprigs of dill
50g (1¾oz) salmon roe
1 slice of smoked salmon, cut into strips
Lamb's lettuce or herb salad

Put four good-sized moulds into the freezer. Steam the salmon steaks for 5 minutes, then remove any bones. Bring to the boil 250ml (9fl oz) water with the fish stock cubes and reduce for 5 minutes over a high heat. Remove from the heat and add the gelatine that has been softened beforehand in a bowl of cold water for a few minutes. Pour into the bottom of each mould some of the cooled gelatine mixture, a sprig of dill, most of the salmon roe, salmon steaks and strips of smoked salmon. Pour in the rest of the gelatine mixture and refrigerate for 2 hours. Turn out the salmon timbales, scatter a little salmon roe on top of them and serve with lamb's lettuce or herb salad.

TERRINE DU FROID
(SALMON AND FENNEL TERRINE)

(6 servings)

Preparation time: 40 minutes
Cooking time: 45 minutes

You will need a steamer.

600g (1¼lb) fennel, diced
450g (1lb) salmon fillet, without the skin
150g (5½oz) virtually fat-free fromage frais
Salt and black pepper
1 pinch of curry powder
2 egg whites
1 tablespoon dill, very finely chopped

Preheat the oven to 180°C/350°F/Gas 4.
Steam the fennel for 10 minutes. Cut two-thirds of
the salmon into big chunks and the other third into
thin strips. Once the fennel is cooked, drain it, then
whiz in a blender until it becomes a smooth purée. Put
aside 3 tablespoons, then add to the rest of the purée
the fromage frais, salt, pepper, pinch of curry powder
and 1 egg white. Mix together well. Blend the salmon
chunks with the 3 tablespoons of fennel purée. Add
the remaining egg white and season. Line a 1-litre
(1¾ pints) terrine dish with greaseproof paper. Pour
half the salmon purée into it and sprinkle over the dill.

Cover with a third of the fennel purée, then with half the salmon strips. Add more fennel and salmon strips, then add the rest of the fennel. Put in the remaining dill and finish off with a final layer of salmon purée. Cover the dish, place into a bigger dish and fill this *bain-marie* half full with cold water. Bake for 45 minutes.

SAUMON SALSA VERDE SUR LIT DE TOMATES CERISES (SALSA VERDE SALMON ON A BED OF CHERRY TOMATOES)

(2 servings)

Preparation time 15 minutes
Cooking time: 45 minutes

300g (10½oz) cherry tomatoes, halved
2 salmon fillets
2 pinches of fish herbs
1 jar or tin of salsa verde (a Mexican sauce made from green tomatoes and chillies)

Preheat the oven to 200°C/400°F/Gas 6.
Place the cherry tomatoes and the salmon fillets inside a greaseproof paper parcel. Sprinkle over the herbs and cover with the salsa verde. Bake for about 45 minutes (do not add any extra salt as the salsa verde contains salt).

SAUMON AU FENOUIL ET AUX POIREAUX
(SALMON WITH FENNEL AND LEEKS)

(4 servings)

Preparation time: 15 minutes
Cooking time: 25 minutes

4 leeks, cut partially lengthways
2 fennel bulbs, cut into quarters
4 onions, studded with 4 cloves
1 bouquet garni
4 salmon steaks
1 egg

Bring to the boil a generous quantity of salted water and drop the leek, fennel, onions and bouquet garni into the water. Cook over a gentle heat for 10 minutes. Add the salmon steaks and continue cooking for 5 minutes. In the meantime, cook the egg for 10 minutes in boiling water until hard-boiled and chop up finely with a fork. When cooked, drain the fish and vegetables, arrange them on a serving dish, sprinkle over the chopped egg and serve immediately.

SALADE AU SAUMON ET À LA VIANDE DES GRISONS (SALMON AND BRESAOLA SALAD)

(4 servings)

Preparation time: 20 minutes
Cooking time: 2–3 minutes

Mixed green salad
30 slices of bresaola
700g (1lb 9oz) salmon, cut into large cubes
A few pink peppercorns, crushed
A few sprigs of chervil

For the vinaigrette
1 teaspoon olive oil
3 tablespoons balsamic vinegar
Salt and black pepper

Divide the salad equally among the plates. Place the bresaola slices on top of the salad. Make up the vinaigrette. Fry the salmon very quickly in a very hot non-stick frying pan, ensuring the cubes are cooked on every side. Arrange the fish on the plates and drizzle over the vinaigrette. Scatter on top the ground pink peppercorns and sprigs of chervil. Serve immediately.

MOUSSE DE SAUMON FUMÉ
(SMOKED SALMON MOUSSE)

(2 servings)

Preparation time: 15 minutes (plus 2–3 hours
   refrigeration)
No cooking required

125g (4½oz) smoked salmon
275g (9¾oz) virtually fat-free fromage frais
1 gelatine leaf
1 teaspoon tomato purée
Juice of 1 lemon
1 pinch of paprika
2 egg whites
4 sticks of celery

Blend the smoked salmon and fromage frais in a blender or food processor to obtain a fine texture. Soak the gelatine leaf in a bowl of cold water for a few minutes, then mix with a spoonful of hot water to dissolve and add this to the mixture. Mix together the tomato purée and lemon juice along with the paprika. Work this into the smoked salmon mixture, whisking them together, and then finally fold in the stiffly beaten egg whites. Pour into ramekin dishes, then refrigerate for 2–3 hours. Serve with the celery sticks.

TERRINE DE CONCOMBRE ET SAUMON FUMÉ (SMOKED SALMON AND CUCUMBER TERRINE)

(2 servings)

Preparation time: 1 hour 15 minutes
No cooking required

1 cucumber
Salt and black pepper
½ bunch of chives, finely chopped
200g (7oz) smoked salmon, cut into very thin slices
200g (7oz) virtually fat-free cottage cheese

Peel the cucumber and cut it in half lengthways. Remove the seeds. Cut the cucumber into small cubes and sprinkle with salt. Cover with clingfilm and place in the fridge for 30 minutes. Stir the chives into the salmon, add pepper (but not salt as the smoked salmon already contains salt). Drain the cottage cheese over a bowl. Drain the diced cucumber and rinse several times. Dry on some muslin or kitchen paper, then add to the salmon-chive mixture. Beat the drained cottage cheese and stir it into the salmon mixture. Adjust the seasoning and refrigerate for at least 30 minutes before serving.

PAPILLOTES DE SAUMON AUX LÉGUMES (BAKED SALMON AND VEGETABLE PARCELS)

(4 servings)

Preparation time: 20 minutes
Cooking time: 20 minutes

1 small courgette
2 tomatoes
4 salmon steaks
100g (3½oz) button mushrooms, thinly sliced
1 lemon, cut into quarters
Salt and black pepper
2 teaspoons pink peppercorns

Preheat the oven to 220°C/425°F/Gas 7.

Thinly slice the courgette, without removing its skin. Poach the tomatoes in boiling water for 30 seconds, then peel and deseed them and cut into quarters. Place the salmon steaks onto sheets of greaseproof paper. Arrange the vegetables around the salmon, along with the lemon quarters. Season with salt and pepper, then scatter over a few pink peppercorns. Carefully seal the parcels and place them in a baking dish. Cook for 20 minutes.

PAVÉS DE SAUMON À LA MENTHE (MINTED SALMON)

(4 servings)

Preparation time: 20 minutes (plus 12 hours refrigeration)
Cooking time: 30 minutes

500g (1lb 2oz) salmon fillet
1 large courgette, thinly sliced lengthways, leaving the skin on
3 drops of oil
2 gelatine leaves
1 slice of smoked salmon, cut up
1 tablespoon virtually fat-free fromage frais
2–3 tablespoons mint, chopped
Salt and black pepper

Wrap the salmon fillet in foil and either steam it or bake it in a medium oven for 30 minutes. Leave to cool, then roughly chop. Quickly brown the courgette in a non-stick frying pan (oiled and wiped with kitchen paper), over a fairly high heat. Soak the gelatine leaves in a bowl of cold water for a few minutes, then heat in a saucepan with a tablespoon of water to dissolve. Work the gelatine into the salmon, smoked salmon, fromage frais and mint. Mix everything together well and season with salt and pepper. Line four ramekin dishes with the courgettes slices and pour in the salmon mixture. Refrigerate for 12 hours and remove from the fridge 30 minutes before serving.

COLIN FARCI
(HAKE STUFFED WITH CRAB AND TOMATO)
(4 servings)

Preparation time: 15 minutes
Cooking time: 30 minutes

50g (1¾oz) onion, chopped
25g (1oz) celery, chopped
1 tablespoon parsley, finely chopped
100g (3½oz) white crab meat
1 egg
Salt and black pepper
250ml (9fl oz) tomato juice
800g (1lb 12oz) hake, cut into 8 slices

Preheat the oven to 220°C/425°F/Gas 7.
To make the stuffing, mix together with a spatula the onion, celery, parsley, crab and egg, then season. Spread this stuffing mixture over four of the fish slices and cover with the other four slices. Place in a small casserole dish. Pour the tomato juice over the fish and bake for 30 minutes. Serve piping hot.

MASALA DE BAR
(MASALA SEA BASS AND SCAMPI)

(4 servings)

Preparation time: 15 minutes (plus 1 hour marinating
  time)
Cooking time: 25 minutes

1 tablespoon garam masala
275g (9¾oz) fat-free natural yoghurt
400g (14oz) sea bass fillet, cut into chunks
200g (7oz) Dublin Bay prawns, shelled
Salt and black pepper
2 shallots, very finely chopped
3 drops of oil
400g (14 oz) carrots, cut into very thin strips
200g (7oz) fennel, cut into very thin strips
2 tablespoons vegetable stock
1 teaspoon cornflour
75g (2¾oz) watercress
Lemon juice

Whisk the garam masala powder into 150g (5½oz) of
the yoghurt. Season the chunks of bass and scampi
with salt and coat them with this yoghurt mixture.
Marinate for at least 1 hour in a cool place. Drain the
fish and scampi on kitchen paper. Fry them over a high
heat for a few moments, then put to one side on a plate
and cover. Next, fry the shallot in a non-stick frying

pan (oiled and wiped with kitchen paper), stirring all the time. Add the carrot and fennel, let them sweat for a few minutes, then pour the vegetable stock over them, cover and cook until the vegetables are tender. Blend the remaining yoghurt with the cornflour and 1 teaspoon cold water. Whisking all the time, pour this yoghurt mixture in with the vegetables and bring to the boil. Then add the cooked fish chunks and Dublin Bay prawns. Arrange on the plate, still warm, with the watercress and the lemon juice, salt and pepper scattered over.

FONDUE CHINOISE (CHINESE FONDUE)

(4 servings)

Preparation time: 25 minutes
Cooking time: 10 minutes

You will need a fondue set.

600g (1¼lb) vegetables of your choice (cabbage, carrots, mushrooms, celery, tomatoes)

400g (14oz) fish (monkfish, cod or sea bream), cut into bite-sized pieces
100g (3½oz) calamari, sliced
12 Dublin Bay prawns or prawns

12 mussels, scrubbed and rinsed well
1 lemon, sliced
1 litre (1¾ pints) fish stock
A few sprigs of chervil

Cook the vegetables separately until *al dente,* either by steaming them or cooking them in an extra 300ml (10fl oz) low-salt strong fish stock. Leave to cool and arrange beautifully on a dish or on the four plates. Place the fish in a dish or on the four plates along with the calamari, scampi and mussels. Garnish with lemon slices. Season the stock so that it tastes nice and strong and add the chervil sprigs. Bring it to the table and place on a lighted fondue heater. Dip the vegetables and fish into the stock until cooked (discard any unopened mussels) and eat with an accompanying seafood sauce, as for a Chinese fondue.

POISSON EN PAPILLOTE
(BAKED FISH PARCELS)

(4 servings)
Preparation time: 20 minutes
Cooking time: 10 minutes

4 slices of lean fish fillet
2 onions, finely chopped
2 tomatoes, finely chopped
2 carrots, finely chopped
1 green pepper, finely chopped
2 stick of celery, finely chopped
2 sprigs of parsley, finely chopped
Salt and black pepper

Preheat the oven to 240°C/475°F/Gas 9.
Place each fish slice onto a sheet of greaseproof paper, then arrange the chopped vegetables on top. Season with salt and pepper. Carefully seal up the fish parcels, turn the oven down to 200°C/400°F/Gas 6 and bake the parcels for 10 minutes.

SALADE D'ÉPINARD AU POISSON FUMÉ
(SPINACH AND SMOKED FISH SALAD)

(4 servings)

Preparation time: 5 minutes
Cooking time: 2 minutes

700g (1lb 9oz) young spinach leaves
300g (10½oz) smoked fish (salmon, trout or eel), cut
    into 2cm (¾ inch) strips
Mustard, to taste
Vinegar, to taste
1 teaspoon hazelnut-flavoured or other vegetable oil
Salt and black pepper

Wash and dry the young spinach leaves and arrange on individual plates. Gently fry the fish for 2 minutes in a frying pan and place on the spinach. Make up a vinaigrette using the mustard, vinegar and hazelnut-flavoured oil and drizzle it all over the fish and spinach. Season with salt and pepper.

BLANQUETTE DE POISSON
(FISH STEW)

(2 servings)

Preparation time: 20 minutes
Cooking time: 20 minutes

500g (1lb 2oz) fish (monkfish, John Dory), cut into chunks
75g (2¾oz) button mushrooms, finely chopped
3 drops of oil
250g (9oz) mussels, scrubbed and rinsed well
250ml (9fl oz) fish stock
½ lemon
2 tablespoons virtually fat-free fromage frais
1 egg yolk
Salt and black pepper

Fry the fish pieces and mushrooms in a non-stick frying pan (oiled and wiped with kitchen paper). As soon as they are golden brown, add the mussels and pour in the fish stock. Cook for 10–15 minutes, then drain the fish, keeping the cooking liquid. Discard any unopened mussels. Shell the rest of the mussels and keep them warm with the fish. Return the cooking liquid to a small pan, reduce the liquid and strain it. Stir in the lemon juice and bind the sauce with the fromage frais and egg yolk over a very gentle heat, without allowing it to boil. Season. Pour this sauce over the fish and vegetables and serve.

TERRINE DE POISSON À LA CIBOULETTE
(FISH AND CHIVE TERRINE)

(3 servings)

Preparation time: 40 minutes (plus overnight draining)
Cooking time: 1 hour

You will need a steamer.

300g (10½oz) spinach
200g (7oz) carrots
400g (14oz) sea bream (or whiting) fillets
4 egg whites
2 tablespoons virtually fat-free fromage frais
Salt and black pepper
300g (10½ oz) salmon fillet, cut into thin strips

For the sauce
150g (5½oz) fat-free natural yoghurt
Juice of 1 lemon
A few sprigs of chives (or tarragon)
Salt and black pepper

Prepare the spinach a day in advance if possible. Cook in a pan of salted boiling water for a couple of minutes. Whiz in a blender, and then leave in a cool place overnight to thoroughly drain.

Preheat the oven to 180°C/350°F/Gas 4.

Steam the carrots for 10 minutes and whiz in a

blender. Blend the sea bream separately with the egg whites, fromage frais, pepper and salt. Divide this mixture into three portions. Stir the blended carrots into one portion, into the second stir the spinach and leave the last portion as it is. In a tin lined with greaseproof paper, build up layers of these different mixtures, separating each layer with the salmon strips. Bake for 45 minutes. To make the sauce, mix together the yoghurt, lemon, herbs and some seasoning and serve with the terrine.

TERRINE MINUTE
(SPINACH AND FISH TERRINE)

(8 servings)

Preparation time: 15 minutes
Cooking time: 40 minutes

550g (1¼lb) white fish fillets
500ml (18fl oz) low-salt fish stock cube
450g (1lb) frozen spinach
Salt and black pepper
2 eggs, separated

Preheat the oven to 220°C/425°F/Gas 7.
Cover and cook the fish in the stock for 10 minutes, first over a high heat, and then over a medium heat. Thaw the spinach, blend it with the drained fish and

season with salt and pepper. Blend the egg yolks with the fish and spinach mixture, then gently fold in the stiffly beaten egg whites. Put in a cake tin, place into a bigger dish and fill this *bain-marie* half full with cold water. Bake for 30 minutes. Serve hot or cold.

Vegetables

ASPERGES ET SAUCE MOUSSELINE
(ASPARAGUS WITH A MOUSSELINE SAUCE)

(2 servings)

Preparation time: 20 minutes
Cooking time: 20 minutes

600g (1¼lb) asparagus
1 low-salt vegetable stock cube
25g (1oz) cornflour
300ml (10fl oz) milk
2 eggs, separated
Salt and black pepper
Juice of 2 lemons

Peel the asparagus and snap off the woody bottom of the asparagus spears at their natural breaking point. Cook in salted, boiling water, flavoured with the stock cube, for 10–15 minutes, until the asparagus stalks are tender. Once the asparagus is cooked, drain it. Prepare the mousseline sauce at the very last moment.

Start by mixing the cornflour in the cold milk, then warm it in a small saucepan over a gentle heat, stirring continuously, until the sauce is smooth. Add the egg yolks. Cook for a further 2 minutes. Season with salt and pepper. Pour the lemon juice into the sauce. Beat the egg whites until stiff and gently fold them in just before serving this dish.

TERRINE D'AUBERGINES
(AUBERGINE CHICKEN TERRINE)

(4 servings)

Preparation time: 25 minutes
Cooking time: 1 hour

2 aubergines, sliced
Salt
100g (3½ oz) cooked chicken or turkey, cut into small, chunky cubes
3 sticks of celery, chopped
3 sprigs of parsley, chopped
1 garlic clove, chopped
3 tomatoes, sliced

Preheat the oven to 180°C/350°F/Gas 4.
Sprinkle some salt over the aubergine and leave to degorge any juices. Brown the chicken cubes in a frying pan. Leave on one side, but keep the juices for the

vegetables. Brown the celery in the frying pan over a gentle heat, then mix together the chicken cubes and celery. In an ovenproof terrine dish, arrange a layer of half the aubergine slices, then add the celery and chicken mixture, parsley, garlic and tomato and finish off with a layer of the remaining aubergine slices. Bake in the oven for 1 hour.

AUBERGINES À L'INDIENNE
(INDIAN-STYLE AUBERGINES)

(2 servings)

Preparation time: 20 minutes
Cooking time: 20 minutes

50g (1¾oz) tomato, cut into small pieces
Salt and black pepper
1 tablespoon herbes de Provence (mixed herbs)
1 pinch of curry powder
1 pinch of paprika
1 pinch of ground coriander
200g (7oz) aubergines, thinly sliced
50g (1¾oz) red pepper, very thinly sliced

Preheat the oven to 220°C/425°F/Gas 7.
Cook the tomato over a gentle heat in a non-stick frying pan. Season with salt and pepper. Add the herbs and spices. Blanch the aubergine and pepper

for a few minutes, then refresh in some cold water. In a baking dish, place a layer of cooked aubergines, then a layer of peppers. Pour the tomato sauce over them and bake for 10 minutes.

AUBERGINES À L'AIL ET AU PERSIL (GARLIC AND PARSLEY AUBERGINES)

(2 servings)

Preparation time: 15 minutes
Cooking time: 35 minutes

200–250g (7–9oz) aubergines
1 garlic clove
2 nice big sprigs of parsley
Salt and black pepper

Preheat the oven to 190°C/375°F/Gas 5.
Remove the stalks from the aubergines and halve them lengthways. Scoop out the flesh, then chop up with the garlic and parsley. Season with salt and pepper and stuff the aubergine halves with this mixture. Wrap each of the aubergine halves in a sheet of aluminium foil and bake for about 30 to 35 minutes.

AUBERGINES À LA CORIANDRE
(CORIANDER AUBERGINES)

(6 servings)

Preparation time: 30 minutes
Cooking time: 45 minutes

5 large aubergines
5 tomatoes, sliced
4 tablespoons finely chopped onion
1 teaspoon chilli powder
Salt and black pepper
2½ teaspoons coriander, very finely chopped

Preheat the oven to 200°C/400°F/Gas 6.

Put three aubergines in some aluminium foil and bake for 30 minutes. Carefully take the aubergines out of the oven, wait 5 minutes for them to cool then, holding them by the bottom part, remove the skin and chop the flesh. In a saucepan of salted water, cook the two remaining aubergines, cut in half lengthways, for 10 minutes over a high heat, then set aside. Put the chopped aubergine, tomato, onion and chilli powder into a frying pan and stir everything together well. Season with salt and pepper and cook over a high heat, stirring occasionally. Scoop the flesh out of the two halved aubergines, leaving 1cm (½ inch) around the edges. Fill them with the chilli mixture and sprinkle the coriander on top. Serve hot or cold.

AUBERGINES À LA PROVENÇALE
(PROVENÇAL AUBERGINES)

(1 serving)

Preparation time: 15 minutes
Cooking time: 45 minutes

1 medium onion, thinly sliced
1 aubergine, cut into cubes
1 tomato, chopped
1 garlic clove, chopped
2 sprigs of thyme
1 tablespoon basil, chopped
Salt and black pepper

Sweat the onion in a non-stick frying pan with a little water until it turns translucent. Add the aubergine and brown it, first over a high heat, then over a medium heat. Add the tomato, garlic, thyme and basil and season with salt and pepper. Cover and simmer for 30 minutes over a gentle heat.

CAVIAR D'AUBERGINE
(AUBERGINE DIP)

(4 servings)

Preparation time: 30 minutes
Cooking time: 15 minutes

6 firm aubergines
2 garlic cloves, crushed
Juice of 1 lemon
1 tablespoon cider vinegar
Salt and black pepper
Olive oil (optional)

Preheat the oven to 220°C/425°F/Gas 7.

Bake the aubergines for about 15 minutes until their skins crackle, turning them over from time to time. Carefully take the aubergines out of the oven, wait 5 minutes for them to cool then, holding them by the bottom part, remove the skin and crush the flesh using either a fork or a liquidizer. Add the garlic, lemon juice and vinegar and season very generously with salt and pepper. If necessary, add a little olive oil, a teaspoon at a time, whisking it in very slowly as if making mayonnaise. Serve very cold.

SALADE D'AUBERGINES
(AUBERGINE SALAD)

(2 servings)

Preparation time: 15 minutes (plus soaking time)
Cooking time: 40 minutes

2 nice aubergines
1 teaspoon cider vinegar
1 teaspoon olive oil
1 garlic clove, crushed
4 spring onions, finely chopped
1 shallot, very finely chopped
2 parsley sprigs, chopped
Salt and black pepper

Peel the aubergines, cut them into large pieces and cook in boiling salted water over a high heat for approximately 20 minutes. Lower the heat and continue cooking for about 20 minutes more. Leave to cool, then crush with a fork. Leave the aubergine to soak in a strong vinaigrette, made from the vinegar, olive oil, garlic, spring onion and shallot. Sprinkle over the parsley, season to taste and serve very cold.

ESTRASSES D'AUBERGINES
(PROVENÇAL AUBERGINE STRIPS)

(4 servings)

Preparation time: 20 minutes
Cooking time: 1 hour 10 minutes

600g (1¼lb) aubergines
2 onions, finely chopped
1kg (2¼lb) tomatoes
2 garlic cloves, crushed
Salt and black pepper

Peel the aubergines and cut them into 1cm (½ inch) thick slices lengthways. In a lightly oiled, small casserole dish, brown the onion over a medium heat. Poach the tomatoes in boiling water for 30 seconds, then peel and chop them. Add the tomato to the onion along with the garlic. Season with salt and pepper. Cover and cook for 30 minutes over a medium heat, then purée the tomato mixture in a liquidizer and return to the casserole dish. Put the aubergine strips into the tomato purée. Cover and gently simmer for a further 30 minutes. Adjust the seasoning before serving.

MOUSSE D'AUBERGINES
(AUBERGINE MOUSSE)

(2 servings)

Preparation time: 40 minutes (plus 6 hours chilling)
Cooking time: 35 minutes

500g (1lb 2oz) aubergines
2 red peppers
2½ tablespoons powdered gelatine
2 tablespoons sherry vinegar
2 garlic cloves, crushed
300g (10½oz) fat-fat natural yoghurt
Salt and black pepper

Preheat the oven to 200°C/400°F/Gas 6.
Bake the aubergines and peppers for about 30 minutes, depending on their size. Leave the gelatine to dissolve in the sherry vinegar for 5 minutes in a small saucepan. Next, warm this over a low heat, stirring all the time. Peel the peppers and remove the stalk and seeds. Cut the aubergines in half and scoop out the flesh with a spoon. Place the garlic, aubergine flesh and peppers in a blender and whiz until puréed. Add the gelatine and yoghurt, season with salt and pepper and mix everything together thoroughly. Pour the mixture into a small terrine dish and leave to set in the fridge for 6 hours.

BLETTES AU TOFU
(SWISS CHARD WITH TOFU)

(4 servings)

Preparation time: 20 minutes
Cooking time: 20 minutes

500g (1lb 2oz) Swiss chard
400g (14oz) spinach
½ onion, finely chopped
250g (9oz) tofu, cut into small cubes
1 teaspoon soy sauce
Salt and black pepper
1 teaspoon mint, very finely chopped

Wash the chard and spinach, drain and chop up. In a non-stick, high-sided frying pan, gently fry the onion until golden brown, then add the spinach and chard, cover and cook for 10 minutes. In the meantime, brown the tofu with the soy sauce in a frying pan for 5 minutes over a very gentle heat. Season with salt and pepper and continue cooking for a further 5 minutes. Serve the vegetables hot with the tofu, sprinkling over the mint.

CHAMPIGNONS À LA GRECQUE
(MUSHROOMS À LA GRECQUE)

(2 servings)

Preparation time: 20 minutes
Cooking time: 15 minutes

5 teaspoons lemon juice
2 bay leaves
1 teaspoon coriander seeds, plus extra for a garnish
1 teaspoon black pepper
Salt
700g (1lb 9oz) button mushrooms, chopped
4 teaspoons flat-leaf parsley, chopped

Pour 500ml (18fl oz) water into a saucepan along with the lemon juice, bay leaves, coriander seeds, pepper and a pinch of salt. Bring to the boil, cover and simmer for 10 minutes. Add the mushrooms to the saucepan, return to the boil and cook for 2 minutes, then turn off the heat. Add the parsley and stir everything together carefully. Leave the mushrooms in the cooking juices until completely cold. Drain the mushrooms, place in a serving dish, pour the cooking juices over them and scatter a few coriander seeds on top.

BALLOTINS DE CHAMPIGNONS (STUFFED MUSHROOM PARCELS)

(6 servings)

Preparation time: 20 minutes
Cooking time: 25 minutes

24 button mushrooms
100g (3½oz) courgettes, finely chopped
2 shallots, chopped
1 garlic clove, chopped
3 drops of oil
150g (5½oz) extra-lean ham, cut into strips
1 red chilli, very finely chopped
1 pinch of breadcrumbs
2 egg yolks
2 tablespoons herbs (parsley, basil, chervil, chives),
   very finely chopped
6 mint leaves
Salt and black pepper
12 chives

Preheat the oven to 220°C/425°F/Gas 7.
Clean the mushrooms, then remove the mushroom tops from their stalks and place them, rounded side up, in a baking dish. Bake in the oven for 5 minutes. Chop up the mushroom stalks. Boil the courgette for 2 minutes in salted water. Brown the shallot and garlic with 1 tablespoon water in a non-stick frying

pan (oiled and wiped with kitchen paper). Add the courgette, ham, chilli and mushroom stalks and cook until all the moisture has evaporated. Remove from the heat and add the breadcrumbs, egg yolks, chopped herbs and mint. Season with salt and pepper. Fill 12 mushrooms with the stuffing mixture, cover them up with the remaining 12 mushrooms, and then tie them up into little parcels with the chives. Bake in the oven for 10 minutes.

TOMATES SALSA
(COOKED TOMATO SALSA)
(2 servings)

Preparation time: 20 minutes
Cooking time: 8 minutes

4 very ripe tomatoes
1 red onion (or white), cut into 8 pieces
2 garlic cloves, crushed
Salt
5 jalapeños, halved
1 tablespoon lemon juice
A few sprigs of coriander

Poach the tomatoes in boiling water for 30 seconds, then peel and deseed them. Chop them up roughly and place in a food processor. Add the onion quarters, garlic and a pinch of salt. Scoop out the insides of the chillies, keeping the seeds or not depending on how hot and spicy you want your salsa to be. Chop them up roughly and add to the food processor with however many seeds you decide on. Blend until the sauce is of a good consistency. Pour the sauce into a saucepan and warm it over a medium heat until it is covered with pink froth (this should take 6–8 minutes). Remove from the heat and leave to cool for at least 10 minutes. Add the lemon juice and coriander.

CHIPS DE TOMATES AU PAPRIKA (PAPRIKA TOMATO CRISPS)

(4 servings)

Preparation time: 10 minutes
Cooking time: 2 hours

10 nice, firm and round tomatoes
A few generous pinches of mild paprika

Preheat the oven to 170°C/325°F/Gas 3.
Cut the tomatoes into 2–3mm (1/8 inch) thick slices. Place them on some greaseproof paper and sprinkle mild paprika powder all over them. Bake for 2 hours. Keep the tomatoes in an airtight container in a dry place.

CHOU BLANC DU NORD
(TERIYAKI CABBAGE)

(2 servings)

Preparation time: 25 minutes
Cooking time: 5 minutes

2 tablespoons soy sauce
1 tablespoon teriyaki sauce
1 garlic clove, crushed
1 teaspoon grated ginger
Salt and black pepper
450g (1lb) white cabbage, thinly sliced
1 onion, thinly sliced
A few sprigs of thyme

Mix together the soy sauce, teriyaki sauce, garlic, ginger and black pepper. Leave these ingredients to rest for at least 5 minutes. In a very hot non-stick frying pan, brown the cabbage, onion, salt (just a little) and thyme for 3–4 minutes over a high heat (the cabbage should remain crunchy), then add the sauce. Continue cooking until the sauce has almost completely evaporated. The vegetables must retain their bite, so you will need to adjust the quantity of sauce depending on how much cabbage there is.

CHOU-FLEUR VAPEUR (STEAMED CAULIFLOWER)

(2 servings)

Preparation time: 10 minutes
Cooking time: 15 minutes

400g (14oz) cauliflower
2 hard-boiled eggs, chopped
Juice of 1 lemon
2 teaspoons parsley, chopped
1 pinch of cumin
Salt and black pepper

Steam the cauliflower for 15 minutes. Place it in a dish and cover with the chopped hard-boiled eggs. Season with the lemon juice, parsley, cumin, salt and pepper.

CRÈME DE CHOU-FLEUR SAFRANÉE (SAFFRON-FLAVOURED CREAM OF CAULIFLOWER)

(4 servings)

Preparation time: 20 minutes
Cooking time: 1 hour

500g (1lb 2oz) cauliflower
750ml (1¼ pints) skimmed milk
2 garlic cloves, peeled
1 pinch of nutmeg
1 pinch of saffron

Salt and black pepper
1 small bunch of chervil

Blanch the cauliflower florets for 5 minutes in a pan of salted, boiling water. Refresh the cauliflower in cold water, then drain. Bring the milk to the boil and add the cauliflower florets and garlic cloves. Cover and simmer gently for 45 minutes. Blend everything in a food processor to obtain a smooth cream, then pour the mixture back into the saucepan and add the nutmeg and saffron. Cook this creamy mixture for 5 minutes over a gentle heat, without a lid. Pour into a hot soup tureen and season with salt and pepper. Scatter over the chervil leaves and serve immediately.

TERRINE DE POIREAUX
(LEEK TERRINE WITH A TOMATO HERB SAUCE)
(6 servings)

Preparation time: 30 minutes (plus a few hours chilling time)
Cooking time: 30 minutes

2kg (4lb 8oz) young leeks
4 tomatoes
1 tablespoon wine vinegar
2 tablespoons herbs, very finely chopped
Salt and black pepper

Clean the leeks, cutting them up in such a way that they fit the length of your terrine dish. Tie the leeks together in small bunches and cook them in salted, boiling water for 20–30 minutes. Drain in a colander and squeeze them to get rid of as much of the cooking water as possible. Line a terrine dish with clingfilm (making a few holes in the clingfilm so that any water can drain away). Arrange the leeks nicely in the terrine dish and press them down firmly. Chill for a few hours, regularly draining off the water. On the same day, poach the tomatoes in boiling water for 30 seconds, then peel them. Blend the tomato flesh with the vinegar and herbs to produce a sauce. Season with salt and pepper. Turn out the terrine and serve it with this sauce.

TERRINE JARDINIÈRE
(GARDEN TERRINE)
(4 servings)

Preparation time: 15 minutes
Cooking time: 35 minutes

500g (1lb 2oz) leeks
900g (2lb) carrots
5 eggs, beaten
125g (4½oz) virtually fat-free fromage frais
Salt and black pepper
100g (3½ oz) extra-lean ham, chopped

Preheat the oven to 190°C/375°F/Gas 5.

Clean the leeks and cook them in salted, boiling water for 20 minutes. Leave them to drain really well for as long as possible. Grate the carrots and blend with the leeks. Mix together the beaten eggs, fromage frais, salt and pepper. Stir in the vegetables and ham, mixing thoroughly, and pour into a rectangular dish. Cover and bake for about 15 minutes, keeping a constant eye on the terrine until it is cooked.

TIAN PROVENÇAL
(PROVENÇAL TIAN)

(6 servings)

Preparation time: 10 minutes
Cooking time: 55 minutes

5 tomatoes, sliced
2 aubergines, sliced
1 courgette, sliced
500g (1lb 2oz) red peppers, deseeded and sliced
2 green peppers, deseeded and sliced
8 garlic cloves
1 pinch of thyme, very finely chopped
1 pinch of savory or oregano, very finely chopped
5 basil leaves, very finely chopped
Salt or black pepper

Preheat the oven to 220°C/425°F/Gas 7.

Arrange the tomato, aubergine and courgette slices around the edges of a baking dish, alternating each vegetable, then place the peppers in the centre along with the unpeeled garlic cloves. Sprinkle over the thyme, savory and basil leaves. Season with salt and pepper. Bake in the oven for 55 minutes (after about half an hour, moisten with a cup of water so that the vegetables do not dry out). Squeeze out the garlic onto the vegetables to serve.

GÂTEAU AUX HERBES DE PRINTEMPS (SPRING HERB CAKE)

(2 servings)

Preparation time: 10 minutes
Cooking time: 30 minutes

500g (1lb 2oz) virtually fat-free cottage cheese
1 tablespoon skimmed milk
2 eggs
50g (1¾oz) sorrel, very finely chopped
50g (1¾oz) basil, very finely chopped
50g (1¾oz) dandelion leaves, very finely chopped
1 pinch of cinnamon
Salt and black pepper

Preheat the oven to 180°C/350°F/Gas 4.

In a bowl, beat together the well-drained cottage cheese, skimmed milk and eggs until the cream is more or less smooth. Add the herbs, cinnamon, salt and pepper. Pour the mixture into either a cake tin or a terrine dish. Bake for 30 minutes. This cake can be eaten either warm or hot.

CROQUETTES DE COURGETTES (COURGETTE CROQUETTES)

(1 serving)

Preparation time: 15 minutes
Cooking time: 4 minutes per batch

2 courgettes
1 egg
4 tablespoons cornflour
Salt and black pepper

Wash, but do not peel the courgettes, then grate them. Put some salt on them (approximately 1 tablespoon) and leave them for one hour to degorge any juices then drain. Add the egg, salt and pepper. Stir in the cornflour to form a solid mixture. Make up little courgette balls, heat a drop of oil in a frying pan and brown the balls on every side, over a medium heat.

PURÉE D'AUBERGINE OU DE COURGETTE (COURGETTE OR AUBERGINE PURÉE)

(1 serving)

Preparation time: 10 minutes (plus 1 hour refrigeration)
Cooking time: 20 minutes

You will need a steamer.

1 tomato
1 courgette or aubergine
1 teaspoon herbes de Provence (mixed herbs)
1 garlic clove, chopped

Poach the tomato in boiling water for 30 seconds, then peel and deseed. Cut the tomato and courgette or aubergine into cubes. Steam for 20 minutes, then whiz in a blender. Add the herbes de Provence and garlic. Refrigerate for 1 hour and eat cold.

COURGETTES À LA MODE PAYSANNE
(PEASANT-STYLE COURGETTES)

(2 servings)

Preparation time: 10 minutes
Cooking time: 20 minutes

250g (9oz) courgettes, peeled, deseeded and thinly
    sliced
100g (3½oz) virtually fat-free fromage frais
1 teaspoon herbes de Provence (mixed herbs)
Salt and black pepper
A few sprigs of parsley, chopped

Preheat the oven to 220°C/425°F/Gas 7.
Steam the courgette until just tender. Arrange the courgette in an ovenproof dish and cover with a sauce made by mixing together the fromage frais and herbes de Provence. Season with salt and pepper and bake for about 10 minutes. When ready to serve, sprinkle with parsley.

COURGETTES AU COULIS DE TOMATES (COURGETTES WITH A TOMATO COULIS)

(2 servings)

Preparation time: 10 minutes
Cooking time: 40 minutes

2 courgettes, cut into cubes
4 tomatoes
1 teaspoon herbes de Provence (mixed herbs)
1 garlic clove, crushed
Salt and black pepper

Put the courgette into a casserole dish. Poach the tomatoes in boiling water for 30 seconds, then peel and deseed them and add them to the courgette with the herbes de Provence. Cover and cook over a gentle heat for 35–40 minutes. Once the courgettes are cooked, add the garlic and season with salt and pepper.

TAJINE DE COURGETTES
(COURGETTE TAGINE)

(2 servings)

Preparation time: 10 minutes
Cooking time: 40 minutes

2 garlic cloves, crushed
1 teaspoon ground cumin
1 teaspoon ground coriander
1 teaspoon garam masala
3 drops of oil
1 low-salt chicken stock cube
2 tablespoons tomato purée
4 courgettes, cut into chunks
Juice of 1 lemon
1 bunch of coriander

Gently fry the garlic and spices for a few minutes in the bottom of a casserole dish (oiled and wiped with kitchen paper). Add 500ml (18fl oz) water, the stock cube, tomato purée and courgette. Cover and cook for 35 minutes over a medium heat. When ready to serve (if possible in a tagine dish), drizzle over the lemon juice and scatter the coriander leaves on top.

EPINARDS TRICOLORES
(TRICOLOUR SPINACH)

(2 servings)

Preparation time: 10 minutes
Cooking time: 15 minutes

400g (14oz) frozen spinach
3 tomatoes, chopped
2 yellow peppers, finely sliced
A few sprigs of thyme
1 bay leaf
Salt and black pepper

Prepare the spinach according to the packet instructions. Put the tomato, pepper, thyme, bay leaf and a cup of water into a casserole dish. Season with salt and pepper. Cover and cook over a gentle heat for 10 minutes, then add the spinach, heat it through and serve piping hot.

MOUSSE DE CONCOMBRE
(CUCUMBER MOUSSE)

(2 servings)

Preparation time: 1 hour 25 minutes (plus 12 hours
   chilling)
No cooking required

4 gelatine leaves
2 cucumbers
Salt and black pepper
100ml (3½fl oz) skimmed milk
400g (14oz) virtually fat-free fromage frais
Grated zest and juice of 1 lemon
1 onion, chopped
A few sprigs of parsley and tarragon, very finely
   chopped

Place the gelatine leaves in a bowl of cold water to
soak. Peel the cucumbers, slice them and sprinkle with
salt. Leave for 1 hour for the cucumber to degorge
its juices, then rinse under cold water and wipe dry.
Warm the milk over a gentle heat and add the drained
gelatine. Blend the cucumber in a food processor,
then mix in the fromage frais, gelatine milk, grated
zest and juice of the lemon, the onion and the parsley
and tarragon. Season with salt and pepper. Pour this
mixture into a non-stick cake tin (or you can line a tin
with clingfilm) and chill for about 12 hours.

341

CURRY DE CONCOMBRE
(CURRIED CUCUMBER)

(4 servings)

Preparation time: 20 minutes
Cooking time: 25 minutes

2 medium cucumbers
1 small chilli, chopped
1 small tablespoon curry powder
4 small tomatoes, roughly chopped into quarters
100ml (3½fl oz) skimmed milk
1 teaspoon cornflour
Salt

Halve the cucumbers lengthways, then cut the halves into 1cm (½ inch) chunks. In a non-stick saucepan, gently fry the chilli with the curry powder. Add the cucumber and cook over a low heat for 10 minutes, then add the tomato to the pan and continue cooking for 10 minutes. In a bowl, mix together the milk and cornflour and pour over the vegetables. Cook for 1–2 minutes until the sauce thickens. Serve hot.

TZATZIKI
(TZATZIKI)
(1 serving)

Preparation time: 10 minutes (plus a few hours
   refrigeration)
No cooking required

½ cucumber
Sea salt
1 garlic clove, very finely chopped
150g (5½oz) fat-free natural yoghurt

Peel and deseed the cucumber, chop it up very finely,
then sprinkle a generous pinch of sea salt over it and
leave for a few minutes to degorge any juices. Then
mix together all the ingredients and refrigerate for
several hours. Serve very cold.

MOUSSE DE POIVRONS
(RED AND YELLOW PEPPER MOUSSE)

(4 servings)

Preparation time: 25 minutes
Cooking time: 15 minutes

1 yellow pepper
1 red pepper
2 tablespoons sweetener
Salt and black pepper
125g (4½ oz) extra-lean ham
200g (7oz) virtually fat-free fromage frais
A few sprigs of parsley, finely chopped

Grill the peppers for 10 to 15 minutes until charred all over. Place in a plastic bag and leave to cool, before peeling away the skin and seeds and cutting them into slices lengthways. Put the peppers in a saucepan of cold water with the sweetener and season with salt and pepper. Bring to the boil and cook for 10 minutes. Drain, then put to one side four pieces, to be thinly sliced and used as a garnish. Blend the rest of the peppers in a food processor with the ham. Dry out this purée over a gentle heat for 5 minutes, then pour it into a bowl and leave to cool. Just before serving, stir the fromage frais into the pepper purée and decorate with the thin pepper slices and a sprinkling of parsley.

SALADE DE PERSIL
(PARSLEY SALAD)

(2 servings)

Preparation time: 10 minutes
No cooking required

1 very large bunch of flat-leaf parsley
1 medium onion, finely chopped
1½ lemons
Salt

Put the parsley leaves and onion into a bowl. Add the pulp of one lemon and the juice of the other half of lemon. Add salt and mix together well. Serve cold. An ideal accompaniment for grilled meats.

SALADE DU BERGER
(SHEPHERD'S SALAD)

(2 servings)

Preparation time: 15 minutes
No cooking required

4 tomatoes, cut into small chunks
2 small cucumbers, cut into small chunks
2 onions, thinly sliced
2 peppers, deseeded and chopped
A few mint leaves, finely chopped

3 sprigs of flat-leaf parsley, finely chopped
 Juice of ½ lemon
1 teaspoon olive oil
Salt and black pepper

Add all the vegetables and herbs to a bowl. Season with the lemon, oil, salt and pepper.

COCKTAIL GARDEN-PARTY
(GARDEN PARTY COCKTAIL)

(1 serving)

Preparation time: 10 minutes
No cooking required

You will need a juice extractor.

150g (5½oz) tomatoes
50g (1¾oz) carrots, peeled
30g (1oz) celery, peeled
Juice of 1 lemon
50ml (2fl oz) water

Poach the tomatoes in boiling water for 30 seconds, then peel and deseed them. Put all the ingredients in a juice extractor and juice. Serve the juice very cold.

COCKTAIL VITALITÉ
(VITALITY COCKTAIL)

(2 servings)

Preparation time: 15 minutes
No cooking required

300g (10½oz) carrots, cut into small pieces
100g (3½oz) celeriac, peeled and cut into small pieces
25g (1oz) dill
1 teaspoon salt

Liquidize the vegetables in the food processor with 400ml (14fl oz) water, the dill and salt for about 45 seconds until the mixture is nice and smooth. Serve very cold.

Desserts

CRÈME AU CHOCOLAT
(CHOCOLATE CREAM)

(4 servings)
Preparation time: 5 minutes
Cooking time: 20 minutes

400ml (14fl oz) skimmed milk
4 pinches of ground cinnamon
20 drops of vanilla extract
4 tablespoons fat-reduced cocoa
4 tablespoons sweetener
4 eggs

Preheat the oven to 200°C/400°F/Gas 6.
Bring to the boil the milk, cinnamon and vanilla. Add
the cocoa and sweetener. Leave to cool. Beat together
the eggs and gradually stir in the warm milk mixture.
Pour this into ramekin dishes. Place the dish into a
bigger dish and fill this *bain-marie* half full with cold
water. Bake for 15 minutes. Serve cold.

CRÈME EXOTIQUE
(CINNAMON CREAM)

(4 servings)

Preparation time: 5 minutes
Cooking time: 10 minutes

1 egg
1 tablespoon cornflour
500ml (18fl oz) skimmed milk
½ teaspoon vanilla extract
¼ teaspoon ground cinnamon
1 teaspoon rum (optional)
2 tablespoons sweetener
1 egg white

In a bowl, whisk together thoroughly the whole egg and the cornflour and mix in 100ml (3½fl oz) of the cold milk. Pour the rest of the milk into a small saucepan and bring to the boil. Whisking continuously, add it to the cornflour mixture and pour this all back into the saucepan. Warm over a gentle heat, stirring continuously with a wooden spoon. As soon as it starts to boil, the cream will be set. Remove it immediately from the heat and pour it into a very cold shallow bowl. Add the vanilla, cinnamon and rum, then the sweetener. Mix together thoroughly. Beat the egg white until stiff, then gently fold it into the cream whilst it is still warm. Serve cold.

DANETTE
(DANETTE)

(4 servings)

Preparation time: 15 minutes
Cooking time: 5 minutes

1 litre (1¾ pints) skimmed milk
3 tablespoons aspartame
2 tablespoons cornflour
2 tablespoons fat-reduced cocoa

Keep aside 150ml (5fl oz) of the milk, put the rest in a saucepan and bring up to the boil. Put the cold milk, sweetener, cornflour and cocoa into a cocktail shaker and thoroughly shake. Once the milk is starting to come to the boil, add the cocktail shaker mixture to the saucepan, stirring all the time. Gently bring this mixture back to the boil, over a low heat, until it just starts to boil. Pour into small ramekin dishes and serve cold.

GÂTEAU AU CHOCOLAT
(FLOURLESS CHOCOLATE CAKES)

(2 servings)

Preparation time: 15 minutes
Cooking time: 15 minutes

3 large eggs, separated
1 tablespoon sweetener
10g (¼oz) fat-reduced cocoa
1 pinch of ground nutmeg

Preheat the oven to 180°C/350°F/Gas 4.
Beat the egg yolks with the sweetener and cocoa. Beat
the egg whites until stiff. Gently fold the egg whites
into the chocolate mixture, add the nutmeg and fill
two ramekin dishes. Bake for 10–15 minutes.

GÂTEAU MOUSSELINE À L'ORANGE
(ORANGE MOUSSELINE CAKE)

(4 servings)

Preparation time: 20 minutes
Cooking time: 20 minutes

1 orange
1 egg
10g (¼oz) aspartame
80g (2¾oz) cornflour
3 tablespoons sweetener
6 teaspoons crème fraîche (less than 5% fat) (optional)
3 egg whites

Preheat the oven to 180°C/350°F/Gas 4.
Rinse the orange under hot water, then grate enough of the skin to get 2 teaspoons of zest. Squeeze the orange and put the juice to one side. Beat the whole egg with the aspartame until it is frothy and light. Add the cornflour, sweetener and crème fraîche. Pour in the orange juice and zest. Mix together thoroughly. Beat the egg whites until stiff and gently fold them into the mixture. Pour into a non-stick sandwich tin and bake for 20 minutes.

MERINGUES
(CHOCOLATE AND COFFEE MERINGUES)

(Makes approximately 12 meringues)

Preparation time: 10 minutes
Cooking time: 20 minutes

3 egg whites
2 teaspoons fat-reduced cocoa
6 tablespoons aspartame
2 teaspoons very strong coffee

Preheat the oven to 150°C/300°F/Gas 2.
Beat the egg whites until very stiff. Add the cocoa to the sweetener, then sprinkle this over the egg whites (so that the egg whites remain stiff, only add the sweetener once the egg whites are already nice and stiff). Add the coffee and continue beating for about 30 seconds. Divide the mixture into small piles on a baking tray and bake for 15–20 minutes.

GLACE ALLÉGÉE
(LOW-FAT ICE CREAM)

(4 servings)

Preparation time: 15 minutes
No cooking required

90g (3oz) virtually fat-free fromage frais
90g (3oz) virtually fat-free quark
3 egg yolks
1 tablespoon crème fraîche (less than 5% fat)
   (optional)
75g (1¾oz) aspartame
Flavouring of your choice (coffee, reduced-fat cocoa,
   vanilla, lemon zest, cinnamon)
2 egg whites

Beat the fromage frais, quark, egg yolks, crème fraîche, aspartame and flavouring of your choice together, vigorously, for 2 minutes. Whisk the egg whites until stiff, gently fold them into the mixture, pour into an ice tray and freeze.

SOUFFLÉ AU CACAO GLACÉ
(ICED COCOA SOUFFLÉ)

(4 servings)

Preparation time: 10 minutes (plus 3 hours freezing)
No cooking required

60g (2¼ oz) fat-reduced cocoa
200g (7oz) virtually fat-free fromage frais
4 egg whites
6 tablespoons sweetener

Sprinkle the cocoa through a fine sieve into the fromage frais. Beat the fromage frais and cocoa together with an electric hand whisk. Beat the egg whites with the sweetener until stiff. Stir the two mixtures together very carefully. Surround the inside of a soufflé dish with a strip of aluminium foil that should extend at least 3cm (1¼ inches) above the dish. Pour in the mixture, which should come up as far as the aluminium foil. Chill in the freezer for at least 3 hours. Remove the aluminium foil and serve immediately.

NUTELLA DUKAN
(DUKAN NUTELLA)

(1 serving)

Preparation time: 5 minutes
No cooking required

1 egg yolk
1 teaspoon fat-reduced cocoa
2 tablespoons aspartame
A little water

Mix together all the ingredients until smooth.

Sauces and dressings

VINAIGRETTE MAYA
(MAYA VINAIGRETTE)
(Makes 2 portions)

Preparation time: 5 minutes
No cooking required

1 tablespoon Dijon mustard or Meaux à l'ancienne
5 tablespoons balsamic vinegar
1 teaspoon vegetable oil
1 garlic clove
7-8 basil leaves, chopped
Salt and black pepper

Take an old mustard jar and fill it with all the ingredients, mixing very thoroughly. If you like garlic, leave a clove to marinate in the bottom of the jar.

VINAIGRETTE BOUILLON
(VEGETABLE STOCK VINAIGRETTE)

(Makes 2 portions)

Preparation time: 10 minutes
No cooking required

1 low-salt vegetable salt cube
1 level teaspoon cornflour
2 tablespoons vinegar
1 tablespoon Dijon mustard or Meaux à l'ancienne

Dilute the stock cube in 2 tablespoons hot water, add the cornflour, vinegar and mustard, and mix together well.

DUKAN MAYONNAISE
(DUKAN MAYONNAISE)

(Makes 2 portions)

Preparation time: 10 minutes
No cooking required

1 egg yolk
1 tablespoon Dijon mustard
3 tablespoons virtually fat-free fromage frais or quark
1 tablespoon chopped parsley or chives
Salt and black pepper

Put the egg yolk in a mixing bowl and combine with the mustard. Season with salt and pepper and add the herbs. Gradually mix in the fromage frais or quark, stirring continuously. Mayonnaise must be kept chilled.

DUKAN MAYONNAISE II
(DUKAN MAYONNAISE II)
(Makes 2 portions)

Preparation time: 10 minutes
Cooking time: 10 minutes

1 egg
55g (2oz) virtually fat-free fromage frais or quark
½ teaspoon Dijon mustard
Salt and black pepper

Cook the egg for 10 minutes in boiling water until hard-boiled. Crush with a fork and mix into the fromage frais or quark. Then add the mustard, salt and pepper, and some herbs if you wish. Mayonnaise must be kept chilled.

SAUCE RAVIGOTE
(RAVIGOTE SAUCE)

(Makes 4 portions)

Preparation time: 10 minutes
Cooking time: 10 minutes

1 egg
3 medium gherkins, finely diced
1 small onion, chopped
2 tablespoons each of chopped chives, parsley and
   tarragon
300g (10½oz) fat-free natural yoghurt
½ teaspoon Dijon mustard
Salt

Cook the egg for 10 minutes in boiling water until hard-boiled. In a glass bowl mix together the egg, gherkin, onion and herbs. Add the yoghurt, mustard and salt. Serve with fish, hard-boiled eggs, meat and vegetables.

SAUCE À L'ÉCHALOTE
(SHALLOT SAUCE)

(Makes 10 portions)

Preparation time: 10 minutes
Cooking time: 10 minutes

12 shallots, chopped
125ml (4fl oz) cider vinegar
13 tablespoons skimmed milk
1 egg yolk
Salt and black pepper

Place the shallots in a saucepan with the vinegar and boil for 10 minutes. Remove from the heat and add the milk and beaten egg yolk, stirring vigorously, then add salt and pepper to taste.

SAUCE À L'OIGNON
(ONION SAUCE)

(Makes 10 portions)

Preparation time: 10 minutes
Cooking time: 2 minutes

1 large onion, very finely chopped
125ml (4fl oz) vegetable stock
1 egg yolk
30g (1oz) virtually fat-free fromage frais and quark
    mixed together
1 tablespoon vinegar
1 teaspoon mustard
Salt and black pepper

In a saucepan, cook the onion in the stock for 2 minutes over a medium heat. Mix together the egg yolk, fromage frais and quark mixture, vinegar, mustard and some salt and pepper in a bowl. Once the stock has cooled down, gradually add it to the mixture, stirring thoroughly.

SAUCE AU FROMAGE BLANC (FROMAGE FRAIS AND FENNEL SAUCE)
(Makes 2 portions)

Preparation time: 10 minutes
No cooking required

100g (3½ oz) virtually fat-free fromage frais
Juice of ½ lemon
Salt and black pepper
2 small onions, chopped as finely as possible
½ fennel bulb, very finely chopped
1 teaspoon basil (or parsley), chopped

Mix together the fromage frais and the lemon juice. Season with salt and pepper. To this, add the onion, fennel and basil. Mix everything together thoroughly and store in the fridge until ready to serve.

SAUCE AU POIVRON
(RED PEPPER SAUCE)

(Makes 2 portions)

Preparation time: 15 minutes (plus 1 hour resting)
No cooking required

1 red pepper, deseeded and cut into very thin slices
1 garlic clove, chopped
½ onion, chopped
1 small chilli, finely chopped
Juice of 1 lemon
Salt and black pepper
A few drops of Tabasco

Mix the red pepper, garlic, onion, chilli and lemon juice together carefully, then add the salt, pepper and a few drops of Tabasco. Allow the sauce to rest for at least an hour before serving it.

SAUCE AU SAFRAN
(SAFFRON SAUCE)

(Makes 2 portions)

Preparation time: 2 minutes
No cooking required

1 teaspoon cornflour
1 ladleful of fish stock, at room temperature
A few saffron threads
Salt and black pepper

Mix the cornflour into the fish stock until it has dissolved, then add the saffron. Season with salt and pepper.

SAUCE AUX CÂPRES
(CAPER SAUCE)

(Makes 5 portions)

Preparation time: 10 minutes
Cooking time: 15 minutes

2 tablespoons tomato purée
4 tablespoons skimmed milk
7 cornichons (small gherkins), chopped
12 capers
Salt and black pepper

Mix together the tomato purée and milk. Add 100ml (3½fl oz) water and the gherkins. Boil for 15 minutes, then add the capers, salt and pepper. Serve straight away.

SAUCE AUX ÉPINARDS
(SPINACH SAUCE)

(Makes 4 portions)

Preparation time: 10 minutes
No cooking required

100g (3½oz) spinach
2 tablespoons fat-free natural yoghurt
200ml (7fl oz) low-salt chicken stock
Salt
1 pinch of grated nutmeg

Wash the spinach and quickly blanch it in salted boiling water. Drain, and then blend it in a food processor or chop finely. Add the yoghurt, then gradually stir in the chicken stock. Cook for 1 minute over a high heat. Add salt and the grated nutmeg.

SAUCE AUX FINES HERBES
(HERB SAUCE)

(Makes 2 portions)

Preparation time: 15 minutes
Cooking time: 2 minutes

2 teaspoons cornflour
2 garlic cloves, finely chopped
2 shallots, finely chopped
2 tablespoons virtually fat-free fromage frais
3 sprigs of parsley, finely chopped
3 sprigs of tarragon, finely chopped
4 chives, finely chopped
Salt and black pepper

Blend the cornflour in 100ml (3½fl oz) water and, along with the garlic and shallot, add it to the fromage frais. Heat over a gentle heat for 2 minutes and add the herbs at the very last minute. Season with salt and pepper.

SAUCE BLANCHE
(WHITE SAUCE)

(Makes 3 portions)

Preparation time: 15 minutes
Cooking time: 3 minutes

250ml (9fl oz) chicken stock
2 tablespoons skimmed milk
1 tablespoon cornflour
Salt and black pepper
1 pinch of nutmeg

Mix together the cold stock and milk and gradually blend the cornflour into the liquid. Warm it over a gentle heat until the mixture starts to thicken, stirring it slowly with a wooden spatula. Then remove from the heat, season with salt and pepper and add the grated nutmeg.

SAUCE CHINOISE
(CHINESE-STYLE SAUCE)

(Makes 2 portions)

Preparation time: 15 minutes
No cooking required

1 teaspoon wine vinegar
1 teaspoon mustard
1 pinch of ginger
1 lemon
1 onion, very finely chopped
Salt and black pepper

Mix together the vinegar, mustard and ground ginger.
Add the lemon juice and onion, stirring all the time.
Season with salt and pepper.

SAUCE CITRON
(LEMON AND CHIVE SAUCE)
(Makes 4 portions)

Preparation time: 10 minutes
No cooking required

Juice of ½ lemon
150g (5½oz) fat-free natural yoghurt
1 bunch of chives, finely chopped
Salt and black pepper

Stir the lemon into the yoghurt. Add the chives to the
sauce and season with salt and pepper.

SAUCE CURRY
(CURRY SAUCE)
(Makes 4 portions)

Preparation time: 10 minutes
No cooking required

1 egg
½ onion, finely chopped

Recipes With Proteins And Vegetables

1 teaspoon curry powder
150g (5½oz) fat-free natural yoghurt

Cook the egg for 6 minutes in boiling water, then shell it and remove the yolk. Mix the onion together with the crushed egg yolk and curry powder. Gradually mix in the yoghurt, stirring all the time.

SAUCE DE PAPRIKA AUX POIVRONS (PAPRIKA AND RED PEPPER SAUCE)
(Makes 8 portions)

Preparation time: 15 minutes
Cooking time: 45 minutes

1 red pepper
1 yellow pepper
4 tomatoes
1 onion, peeled
1 teaspoon aspartame
100ml (3½fl oz) wine vinegar
1 pinch of paprika
Salt and black pepper

Grill the peppers for 10 to 15 minutes until charred all over. Place in a plastic bag and leave to cool, before peeling away the skin and seeds. Poach the tomatoes in boiling water for 30 seconds, then peel and deseed them. Blend all the ingredients together in a food processor. Strain and pour the sauce into a saucepan. Cover and cook over a gentle heat for 40 minutes.

SAUCE GRELETTE
(SAUCE GRELETTE)
(Makes 6 portions)

Preparation time: 10 minutes
No cooking required

4 tomatoes
100g (3½oz) virtually fat-free fromage frais
5 shallots, chopped
Juice of 1 lemon
Salt and black pepper

Poach the tomatoes in boiling water for 30 seconds, then peel them. Blend all the ingredients in a food processor. Check the seasoning and serve very cold.

SAUCE GRIBICHE
(GRIBICHE SAUCE)
(Makes 8 portions)

Preparation time: 10 minutes
No cooking required

1 teaspoon mustard

1 tablespoon cider vinegar

Salt and black pepper

1 teaspoon tarragon or vegetable oil

250g (9oz) virtually fat-free fromage frais

2 hard-boiled eggs, chopped

1 shallot, chopped

3 cornichons (small gherkins), finely diced

A few sprigs of tarragon

Put the mustard, vinegar, salt and pepper in a bowl and emulsify by adding the oil slowly. Gradually add the fromage frais, then the hard-boiled eggs, shallot, cornichons and tarragon leaves. Adjust the seasoning to taste.

SAUCE HOLLANDAISE
(HOLLANDAISE SAUCE)

(Makes 2 portions)

Preparation time: 15 minutes

Cooking time: 5 minutes

1 egg, separated

1 teaspoon mustard

1 tablespoon skimmed milk

1 teaspoon lemon juice

Salt and black pepper

Put the egg yolk, mustard and milk in a bowl in a *bain-marie* or by placing the bowl over a pan of simmering water. Whisk vigorously until the sauce thickens without curdling. Remove from the heat whilst continuing all the time to beat the sauce, and add the lemon juice and black pepper. Beat the egg white until stiff and carefully fold into the sauce. Adjust the seasoning.

SAUCE LYONNAISE
(LYONNAISE SAUCE)
(Makes 5 portions)

Preparation time: 10 minutes
No cooking required

125g (4½oz) virtually fat-free fromage frais
1 tablespoon wine vinegar
Salt and black pepper
1 garlic clove, very finely chopped
1 shallot, very finely chopped

Beat the fromage frais with the vinegar and season with salt and pepper. Add the garlic and shallot and whisk until the sauce is evenly blended.

SAUCE MOUTARDE
(MUSTARD SAUCE)

(Makes 8 portions)

Preparation time: 10 minutes
Cooking time: 5 minutes

2 teaspoons cornflour
1 hard-boiled egg yolk
2 teaspoons vinegar
2 teaspoons mustard
A few herbs, to taste
Salt and black perpper

Mix the cornflour with a tablespoon of cold water. Whisk this cornflour paste into 200ml (7fl oz) water as it comes to the boil in a small saucepan. Turn down the heat and simmer for a few minutes, then leave to cool. Blend the egg yolk with the vinegar and mustard and work this into the diluted cornflour. Finally, add the herbs, salt and pepper. If the sauce does not seem runny enough, add some more vinegar.

SAUCE PORTUGAISE
(PORTUGUESE SAUCE)

(Makes 6 portions)

Preparation time: 10 minutes
Cooking time: 30 minutes

8 tomatoes
6 garlic cloves, crushed
2 medium onions, very finely chopped
2 bay leaves
Herbes de Provence (mixed herbs)
Salt and black pepper
1 tablespoon tomato purée
1 green pepper, cut into very thin strips
A pinch of chilli powder (optional)

Cook the tomatoes over a high heat for 10 minutes with the garlic, onion, bay leaves and a few pinches of herbes de Provence. Season with salt and pepper, add the tomato purée and pepper and reduce the sauce for about 20 minutes over a low heat. Remove the bay leaves and blend in a food processor, adding a pinch of chilli powder according to taste.

SAUCE BÉCHAMEL
(BÉCHAMEL SAUCE)

(Makes 6 portions)

250ml (9fl oz) cold skimmed milk
1 tablespoon cornflour
1 low-fat beef bouillon cube
Salt, black pepper and nutmeg

In a saucepan, mix together the cold milk and cornfl our, then add the bouillon cube. Let this cook for a few minutes on a low heat until it thickens. Add salt, pepper and nutmeg to taste. Ideal for vegetable gratins and chicory wrapped in ham during the cruising stage.

INDEX

Index

Index

Index

Index

Index

Index

Index

Index

Index

Index